HIP SANTA CRUZ

Also by Ralph H. Abraham

Chaos, Gaia, Eros
Chaos, Creativity, and Cosmic Consciousness
The Evolutionary Mind
Demystifying the Akasha
Bolts from the Blue

Hip Santa Cruz

First-person Accounts
of the Hip Culture
of Santa Cruz, California
in the 1960s
Edited by Ralph H. Abraham
with the assistance of
Judy Lomba

Epigraph Books
Rhinebeck, New York

For information contact:
Epigraph Publishing Service
22 East Market Street, Suite 304
Rhinebeck, New York 12572
www.epigraphPS.com
Printed in the United States of America

ISBN 978-1-944037-38-3
Library of Congress Control Number: 2016944768
Bulk purchase discounts for educational or promotional purposes are available. Contact the publisher for more information.

CONTENTS

PREFACE

In the 1960s, Santa Cruz was a fountainhead of Hip culture. When I arrived in 1968 to join the new university, UCSC, the creative time was nearly over. By 1980, it seemed to me it had been such a miracle that its birth should be recorded. So I created the Santa Cruz Hip History Project in 2002, collecting oral histories and photographs in a website. This book is a compact summary of the 14 years accumulation of material from that website that was most relevant to the creation of the Hip culture of Santa Cruz. From 1964 to 1970, we will follow the stories of some of the main characters of the Hip miracle in Santa Cruz. These are primarily edited transcripts of interviews and verbal story telling. I chose the people that I personally knew as key characters in the Hip culture. And some of the important innovators of the 1960s have been unfortunately overlooked. I am sorry that most of the voices are male, but our time — preceding the gender equality movement of the 1970s — was predominantly patriarchal.

And I am very grateful for the support of our 11 contributors. During the 14-year incubation of this book, four of these old friends have passed on: Bob, Leon, Max, and Peter. Much more information may be found on our two websites and in the wonderful book by Holly Harman (see the References section.)

Here is a brief chronology of the main events of the time.[1]

- **1958.** The Sticky Wicket, a cafe and gallery on Cathcart Street, was said to be the first Hip hangout. Later it moved to Aptos.

- **1960.** Ken Kesey moved from the Wallace Stegner writing program at Stanford to La Honda. and began house parties, along with LSD, fluorescent paintings, strobe lights, and music. Later, the house band became the Grateful Dead.

---

[1]Many thanks to the UCSC McHenry Library Special Collections for help with this.

- **1961.** Peter Demma, discharged from military service, moved to Palo Alto, met Ken Kesey and Neal Cassady.

- **1962.** Leon Tabory, psychiatrist, moved into Neal Cassady's house in Los Gatos, and opened an office in Santa Cruz. Kesey published *One Flew Over the Cuckoo's Nest.*

- **1963.** Peter, while running a bookstore in San Diego, visited Big Sur. In the hot baths with Ron Bevirt a plan was hatched to open a bookstore in Santa Cruz called the Hip Pocket Bookstore. The sign was to be made by Ron Boise, a sculptor living in Big Sur in a bread truck. A set of his works called the Kama Sutra sculptures was then showing at the Sticky Wicket.

- **1964. Beginning of the golden years.**

  - Ken Kesey published *Sometimes a Great Nation*, formed the Merry Pranksters. The bus Further took them to New York for a Kesey book event. Neal, Ron Bevirt, Lee Quarnstrom, Stewart Brand, Ed McClanahan. and others were on the trip.

  - Peter and Ron Bevirt opened the Hip Pocket Bookstore on September 13 in the St. George Hotel. The Ron Boise sign and two nude sculptures (covered by a sheet) were on hand. Norman Lezin, the mayor of Santa Cruz, had agreed to unveil the sculptures at the opening, which was busted by the police.

  - Later, Neal and Leon used to hang out and help out at the bookstore. Neal suggested the bookstore have free speech night every friday. Leon started them off, speaking about marijuana.

  - Leon hears Eric '"Big Daddy"' Nord was opening the Loft, a cafe at a barn in Scotts Valley. Leon went there, met Cathy, they married.

- 1965.

- November 21, Wavy Gravy's Lysergic A GO GO in LA , with light show by Del Close.[2]
- November 27, the first Acid Test, in Soquel, near Santa Cruz.
- UCSC opened in the Fall.
- Page Stegner joined the faculty at UCSC.
- The Hip Pocket Bookstore closed. Ron Lau purchased the books.

- **1966.**

  - Bookshop Santa Cruz opened by Ron Lau.
  - In the summer, the Barn opened in Scotts Valley by Leon. It featured dances similar to the acid tests, with fluorescent wall paintings by Joe Lysowski and Pat Bisconti. Great artists such as Janis Joplin and Country Joe performed there. A local band performed on musical sculptures created by Ron Boise. Light shows created by Joe were among the first in the US.
  - Paul Lee (philosopher, founding editor of *The Psychedelic Review*) joined UCSC.
  - In the Fall, the Catalyst Coffee House and Delicatessen, run by Al And Patti DiLudovico, opened in the St. George Hotel next to the Bookshop.

- **1967.**

  - Jefferson Airplane played in Santa Cruz.
  - Hippies moved into the Holiday Cabins in Ben Lomond.[3]

- **1968.**

---

[2]See www.rollingstone.com/music/news/acid-tests-turn-50-wavy-gravy-merry-prankster-ken-babbs-look-back-20151130

[3]See Harman, Holly, *Inside a Hippie Commune* (2015) for the full story.

- Spring, I visited UCSC and the Barn, and decided to join UCSC.

- Fall, I arrived with family. Moved into a 24-room Victorian mansion at 724 California Street.

- **1969.**

  - The Barn closed.

  - The Catalyst closed.

  - Jack Kerouac died.

  - I got into trouble at UCSC for political actions, along with Paul Lee.

- **1970. The end of the golden years.**

  - February 26. In the local alternative newspaper, the *Free Spaghetti Dinner*, I wrote in my regular column "Scientific Advice on the Politics of Life," under my pseudonym, Dr. Abraham Clearquill:

    > Last Fall I felt that the emerging community in Santa Cruz was at a watershed, and that a development of some importance to the world was possible. Now I am convinced that this opportunity has passed, and the old structure is being recreated.[4]

  - June, we vacated the Victorian mansion.

Ralph Abraham; June 5, 2016; Bonny Doon, California

---

[4]Thanks to Rick Gladstone, founding editor of the FSD, for recalling this.

Part I

Overview, 1960

1. Pat Bisconti

I interviewed Pat in a cafe on February 26, 2016. The recording was then transcribed by Becky Luening, and edited by Pat and by Judy Lomba.

Pat: I was born in Youngstown, Ohio, on July 18, 1945. My father, back from Europe after serving in the US Army during WWII, worked in a steel mill. When I was five my family moved to the then-beautiful Santa Clara Valley. I went to school in the Campbell – Los Gatos area, and I started hitchhiking by myself over to Santa Cruz when I was about 11. That was probably 1956 or '57. That's when I started coming over to surf on weekends and holidays. I would leave my surfboard with friends at Pleasure Point and hitchhike over until I was able to get my first car; looking back it seems kinda dangerous.

After graduating high school, I went to San Jose State. I was an art major. I went there for two years, got pretty good grades, then quit because I felt they were making me even more stupid; besides, I had other things I wanted to do. I didn't really respect the degree very much, obviously, and probably I made a big career mistake.

But before that, while still in high school, I married my high school sweetheart, Nancy Garthwaite. We were just 17 years old. We've been married 53 years now, and we've had seven kids and 14 grandkids so far. She has been through it all with me, and is my strongest supporter. We were buying a new house in San Jose at that time, and I gave it to my brother.

Santa Cruz

Then we rented a little beach house at Twin Lakes Beach with a cabin in the back by the Lagoon to use as a studio, and we moved to Santa Cruz. This studio cabin is where my friend, and an extremely gifted artist, Steve Sprague, and I created the original manuscript for *The Madjic Trip*, a book about the basic five senses for very young children. A limited first edition in hard and softbound was later published by Madjic Books, at Big Trees Press in Felton, California. I have recently made a newly designed and formatted version of *The Madjic Trip* for unlimited editions, which is presently unpublished. Shortly after we moved there, Sharon Cadwallader and her son Leland moved into a cottage behind us. She later wrote *The Whole Earth Cookbook* and several other books and articles.

Not long after that, Max Hartstein, a New York artist, musician, film-maker, and psychic alchemist moved in with Sharon. He had been living and working in his studio in Mexico. We soon became friends and began collaborating on projects. Phil Hefferton was one of the original New York Pop Artists, and he moved into the neighborhood. I think Max enticed him to come to Santa Cruz. He spent a lot of time hanging out and playing music at our house.

Also Charlie Nothing, another New York artist and musician, migrated to the Twin Lakes Beach area. He had just released a long playing record album on Takoma Records titled *The Psychedelic Saxophone of Charlie Nothing*, which caused much controversy in the Jazz world, as nobody had heard anyone blow so free and relentless.

His friend, Tox Drohard, who was a master of rhythm, especially trap drums and conga drums, arrived at about the same time. He would play for hours at a time, and the ladies loved him. Later, he settled in Paris, France. At that time Joe Lysowski, an important Santa Cruz artist, lived in the neighborhood next to Tony Maggi, another artist and commercial fisherman.

Also Gary Dunn, an all around good guy and musician lived near by. Gary helped metal sculptor Ron Boise by storing Ron's sculptures, and transporting them in his old painted Rio truck.

Also, Stan Fullerton, a very unique artist, was living and painting in Santa Cruz in a regal victorian on top of the hill near the Boardwalk. I still have one of his canvases titled, Ba Ba Yaga and his Cow Kite, an oil painting of a little boy in a field holding a flying cow by the tail, like in the Russian folktale.

All these very creative individuals, and so many more great spirits, were around at that time. In other places, locally and far away, similar ideas and feelings were being manifest. But Santa Cruz, the Monterey Bay area, and Big Sur were definitely hot spots, and they still are. Remember, this was before computers and cell phones, the internet, black holes, space telescopes, etc. This was tape recorders, film, typewriters, the Beatles, Dylan, and lots of old modern technology. The world was changing about that time, I don't think we changed it, but it did change, and we were a part of that. I think of it as an organic natural radical change, like a caterpillar changing into an eagle.

So, around 1964 we were living in this two bedroom house for $70 a month right across the street from the beach and that little lagoon at Schwann Lake. There was a studio cabin behind a row of these other cabins, and I got that for an extra $5 a month, and so that became my art studio, where I worked on *The Madjic Trip* graphics.

Max

Max had come to Santa Cruz from Mexico and that's where and when I met him. He was developing his Paradise Pageant idea, and got me involved in that project for many years. He was also making movies, and I helped him make *Beach Head in Paradise* which we filmed on the 4th of July at the Santa Cruz Boardwalk. He had them all on 16mm, mostly with the soundtracks on separate tapes. It all has to be digitalized and transferred to modern media.

Ralph: I have digital copies of *Beach Head in Paradise* and *The Last Supper*.

Pat: You've got the Boardwalk movie? Okay! That was the first one made in Santa Cruz. That was a lot of fun. Not much of a storyline, more of a social adventure. We shot it all in one day. Later, I started working on *The Space Bass*, Max's documentary about the creation of a machine that actually was able to manipulate time and space and transcend three-dimensional reality. Work on this movie took a couple years and was filmed outdoors.

Ron

I think of this era as the calm before the storm. Things and people who were rather static, became more fluid, active, involved, about that time. Ron Boise had recently caused a large disturbance in the art world with his Kama Sutra sculptures at the Vorpal Gallery in San Francisco. The sculptures begged the question, "What is pornography / What is art?" The city police raided the gallery, took the sculptures, and arrested the relevant people. They had a much publisized court case in San Francisco. We can thank Ron Boise and Allen Watts (who spoke in defense of art and sex at the trial) for fixing that problem.

So Ron was chilling out in Santa Cruz, and in the mountains. He was living and working out of an old bread truck-type vehicle. He had a show at the Hip Pocket Bookstore in Santa Cruz that featured his kinetic sculpture which pointed to the future direction he was taking. He was incorporating electronic things like tape recorders, microphones, looping machines, vacuum cleaners, lights, timers, etc. into the sculptures to have them come alive and move and make noise or whatever. Joe Lysowski had painted most of them, and it was a ground breaking show in that respect.

Then he had an exhibition at the Steam Beer Brewery in San Francisco, which went really well. The large controversial couple sculpture from the Hip Pocket Bookstore in Santa Cruz eventually ended up on the roof of the brewery, where it could be seen from the very busy freeway. A few of us went up to the brewery with Gary Dunn to deliver some of the sculptures, and help set up the show which featured the amazing Thunder Machine painted by Joe Lysowski. The Thunder Machine was a metal sculpture shaped somewhat like a sea shell about 8' x 8' x 10'. The viewer went inside and sat on a seat with a harp-type thing hanging next to it. So the musician was able to be inside the actual sound chamber while playing. There were lights and other features built in also.

That was one of the most enjoyable art openings, because the brewery offered such a complimentary backdrop for the pieces, or maybe because everybody had a beer buzz. Shortly after that,

Ron took his sculptures to Texas for a show. I think Gary took the Thunder Machine for that one. I remember him saying the folks on Haight Street went nuts when he drove through there, jumping on the truck, and following down the street. However, Ron got real sick in Texas and was flown back. Then for some sad lonely reason he didn't recover, or survive.

And for me, this event marked the beginning of the end of the first phase of Flower Power. But, somehow, through Gary, I inherited Ron's welding gauges and some miscellaneous tools. His leather welding gloves had holes burnt in every finger and thumb. I had them hanging in my studios as a rememberence for 30 years, at least. When I completed "The Space Bass", I gave Ron's welding gauges to Charlie Nothing, after teaching him to weld. I wanted to help him get started making his Dingulator Suite, and he became a master metal sculptor himself, with his unique style. All of Ron's and Charlie's pieces are amazing and should be in a museum before they get lost.

So, I had started working on the Space Bass, which I made out of a WWII bomber gas tank that was of good resonating steel. I had been inspired by Ron's Void Harp, but he was making his instruments out of copper, and copper really doesn't resonate very well; it has a dull sound compared to American automobile steel. I was welding sculptures out of metal things I recycled: cars, metal appliances, etc. My family was from Youngstown, Ohio — from the steel mills — they were all in the steel business, so when they came to Santa Clara in the 1950's they were involved in construction with all the schools, freeway overpasses, big buildings. Therefore, I was kind of expected to go into something having to do with steel, so in college I took sculpture classes and learned how to weld. Then I ended up with Ron's gear and started working on the Space Bass. That turned out to be a two-year project. Max was filming the whole time, and when I finished it, we presented it at a big party at the old Holiday Lodge, the hippie commune in Felton, and he filmed that as part of both that movie, and also as part of another movie he made about the commune.

Holidays Resort

It was basically a row of small cabins and a big house along the San Lorenzo River with some acreage, lots of big redwood trees and a flat open garden area. Very pleasant, near Felton, on Highway 9. Max was making a 16mm documentary about the people living there, and what they were doing. It was a colorful mix of individuals, couples, and families, forming somewhat of a tribe, trying to live the dream. So they were having a Harvest Festival celebration or something, and I was invited to publicly present the Space Bass for the first time there. Max was to film everything, to use in the Commune movie and the Space Bass movie.

From the minute the Space Bass landed at the party it was surrounded by people who had never seen it, but instantly intuitively recognized what it was and started playing it. And that began one continuous song that lasted all day with different people playing it non-stop. It was outside and I think it was amped so it could be heard along with a rock band. Both movies came out very well, but they never were finished. We were working with film and tape at that time, if we had today's digital technology then, we would have used it, and Max would have been able to finish his movies. He was a really excellent moviemaker, but in those days getting through the lab was out of his financial range, not having a producer. Max took his movies as far as he could, and then started a new one.

And eventually we had The World Premiere of The Space Bass at the Straight Theater on Haight Street in San Francisco. The Flower Children were still blooming, and we were there to introduce the Space Bass to the big city, and put on a show. Max had organized a band, and a light show, and a bunch of people. More than a busload of people came up from Santa Cruz to be part of the event. I remember standing on the street in front of the theater with the cold San Francisco wind blowing, before the show and looking at the words "World Premiere of The Space Bass Tonight" on the marquee, and thinking maybe something good might happen. Inside everything was set up, the Space Bass center stage with a light show behind. It all looked and felt solid. There were a lot of people having a good time.

So we started playing music and lights, and the thing really took off in a heavenly way, everybody was dancing and playing music, then all of a sudden — FLASH — after 10 or 15 minutes all the bright house lights went on, and the cops came in from everywhere and pushed us up against the wall and effectively shut us down. I guess somebody had stolen somebody's guitar or something, but it kind of killed our thing.

And that was the way The World Premier of the Space Bass turned out. The Space Bass movie was designed to be shown with a light show on one screen while the commune movie was shown next to it on another screen.

Two movies shown simultaneously side by side in the middle of all these liquid projections. And at one point in time they both became the same movie. One was about the hippie commune, and the other was about the Space Bass, except for one section where they merged into the same scene and then split again back into two movies. Both movies end at the same time in a mind-blowing strobe light explosion and light show.

This was all designed to be part of Max's main major master project, The Paradise Pageant, which was to be a public multimedia event with bands and built around the idea that "we" — the 25th Century Ensemble — had come back in a time bubble from the 25th century to remind everybody they are in Paradise, take care of it, and it will take care of you.

Max wrote *The Proclamation Of Paradise* to explain it all. We then recorded it as a song, and it evolved into about a 20 minute mind fugue. This was played on radio stations on the west and east coasts, and even in Vietnam. It was broadcast selectively and not much, but it was very effective when coming out of a radio, because it distorted time and space, and it was hypnotic. This was before there was any real environmental consciousness, or environmental movement to speak of.

This was even before the song, "Cheeseburger in Paradise." Before that time, there had been the beginnings of a return to the Earth, and a recycle energy taking hold in many places, especially in Santa Cruz.

But we weren't focused on the planet as much as we were concerned with helping humans realize the paradise reality for their own good, and the betterment of everything. I think all the noise we made back then might have stimulated and catalyzed some of that energy into what we have going on today. Although today's politicians have taken over the environmental movement, and are using it as a tool to better control us in the totalitarian nightmare they are creating that they call utopia. They use false science, biased research, and a powerful media to fool the fools who vote for them. So that is kinda disappointing, and not what we wanted, back in the day.

Boulder Creek

Max moved up to Boulder Creek, and I moved up the street from him and we shared a studio on the San Lorenzo River for a couple more years, and worked on several projects individually and together. I made a series of kalimbas and bamboo flutes and metal sculptures there.

This was around 1967, '68, '69 — and we continued our music under the name The 25th Century Ensemble, playing Perfect Music, where there are no wrong notes. Every Thursday night the studio was open to the public to play music together. Many people from different places would show up, always new faces mixed with the usual suspects. Always spontaneous free expression.

I remember the nights during the winter storms best. Max recorded every session, and built a large tape collection of these sociological events. I think one of the best things we did was titled "The Legend of the Indian Dogman" with Max, Futzy Nutzle, Fred McPherson, me, and a few others.

As I remember, it was a winter afternoon in the studio by the river in Boulder Creek. Kinda gloomy, maybe rainy, with a nice wood fire in the pot belly stove. We were seated around the stove, and started the song by first meditating on silence, and the natural sounds of the river and the fire, and proceeded from the silence into this acoustic adventure, which amazed us how perfect it sounded when we heard the tape. The 25th Century Ensemble played what they called "Perfect Music," which they said had no wrong notes, and everybody could play anything and it was perfect, but it rarely sounded perfect. This set was like throwing paint at a canvas and having it turn into the Mona Lisa. It is my number one choice of recordings that I would like to have seen produced from that time. There was talk of making it into an album. Futzy Nutzle did brilliant artwork for the cover. I never heard of it being produced, and I don't know if any copies were made. I never got any copies of anything, and my instruments were involved in a lot of those recordings. I never wanted any copies, or asked for any, nobody did, but Max did make copies for disc jockeys or radio stations.

Ralph: Copies may not exist. I have a small box that arrived after Max died that his daughter had gathered. There are four or five 16mm movie rolls labeled "Protest in San Jose," probably not an art event. And there are some audiotapes, two drawings, and a sketchbook with line drawings by Max in it. That's all that survived as far as I know.

Pat: Yes, Max was very involved in Civil Rights issues, and was a World Peace activist. He actually recorded and filmed everything he could for years. He had shelves full of tapes and his studio was set up as a sound studio so all he had to do was turn on the tape machine to capture the set.

Fred

Fred McPherson is our original environmentalist. He was very involved in many of the paradise projects. He was considered a hard core member of the 25th Century Ensemble, and was always cheerful and positive, and willing to help out. I went with him for long treks into the mountain forests to investigate nature, and he would teach me about plants and insects and animals. He marveled at the bright yellow banana slugs that thrive in the redwood forests, and which later he helped to become the mascot for UCSC.

Fred once tried to get me hired as an art teacher at Pacific High School in the mountains where he taught science. It was a private school built by the students, and later run by them after they rebelled and took it over. Anyway, as part of my interview, Fred wanted me to lead a workshop with some students to paint his classroom in the summer before school started. So I got the materials, and met with a group of very talented kids, and turned them loose, and after a couple days they got the job done, and transformed this new classroom into some kind of statement. I only painted the table they sat around. But as it turned out, the classroom we painted was not the one they were assigning to Fred, and somebody was upset because of an American flag painted over the new blackboard. So I didn't get the job, but I really enjoyed being around the kids and watching them enjoy freedom of expression. Then, when school started that year, I heard the students fired the teachers, and moved into the school, and tried to create a better educational system. I didn't hear what happened after that. Then, Nancy and I bought a little cabin in Zayante, and I kind of spaced out on Max and the 25th Century Ensemble, and took a somewhat different direction.

Charlie

I had been doing things with Charlie Nothing since he came to Santa Cruz, but we only began playing music together publicly after I moved to Zayante. He had moved to Bonny Doon and was living off Empire Grade, on what they called The Bump, which was John Lingemann's property. Charlie was given some acreage on the mountain top, and set up a camp and garden-farm where he lived and worked. He later decided to move this scene further out and off the property, but he still had to pass all the way through the property to get to his camp. It was down in a steep canyon, difficult to get to, and very remote. I once helped him carry beehives down the mountain from where the road stopped to his camp. That was kinda difficult, because it was a long slippery steep goat path, and the hives were full of angry bees. He had to carry all his supplies up and down that dangerous path, and at night it was pitch dark.

After some time, he made the place into a way-off-the-grid living reality. He had goats, chickens, rabbits, dogs, a couple of Arabian horses, a garden of vegetables and bonzai fruit trees, and he developed a gravity flow watering system. He lived in a shelter made of canvas tarps spread over some branches, a little fire pit in the middle, and a dirt floor. It was primitive and very Zen. His biggest problem was mountain lions that roamed the area, and were attracted by his water and animals. Charlie tied bells on the rabbit cages, and in the middle of one night he awoke to the sound of the bells, caused by the rabbits thumping their cages. So Charlie got his 30/30 and a flashlight, and went out to investigate. What he saw was a large mountain lion sitting on top of the cages snarling at him about 15 feet away. Charlie fired, and completely missed the lion. The lion jumped to the ground, growled, and casually sauntered off into the forest. The next morning Charlie was still shook up about what it all meant to the future of his farm. He began improving the place to better be protected, but there wasn't anything that could ever fix the problem really. It was hard to understand how he could have missed hitting the mountain lion, because he was an excellent shot usually. He once shot and hit a chicken hawk that had been harrassing his chickens, from about 100 yards, when it landed in a tree.

Eventually, after years of living on the land he decided to move back to town, and get totally involved in computers. He would take them apart, fix them, rebuild them, and hot rod them. He began writing, printing, and binding a series of books with his own publishing company called Dead Trees Press. And he became a master beekeeper, being a regular writer for the International Bee Journal, and he ran a lucrative stinging insect removal business in Santa Cruz and Monterey. He did a musical Dingulation tour in Europe, and released a CD titled *"My Cuntree Tits of Thee"* shortly before passing of cancer.

Curly

We used to play at the Zayante Club on Sunday afternoons, and at other places, for food and drink, and that went on for several years. Then I was given an art grant to live free in what had been the main house on the Lingemann property. John Lingemann moved farther up the mountain and lived in many different dwellings which he made over the years. One of his homes was carved into the white sandstone, like a cave with a panoramic view of the Monterey Bay. These were actually troubled times because there were wars going on over the land and water between Lingemann and some of his kids.

John Lingemann, we called him Curly, had divided the original 160 acre parcel into several approximately 20 acre parcels, which he gave to his family and various people to try to set up living scenes. Charlie was a major player in the management and direction of how that played out. Gary Dunn, Phil Hefferton, and Joe Klein and their ladies were among several people who made valiant efforts to create sometimes brilliant solutions to the problems of living off the land. But only the most committed made a lasting go of it. After they failed, John would burn their places down.

The thing that was most difficult about living there was that there was only one spring on the 160 acres. It was supposed to be available for everyone to use, so all would have water. But apparently someone in the family deeded it to themselves, and sold the spring property to someone who built a big house, and cut the water off to everyone else. So, besides the difficulty of hauling water up a deeply rutted and washed out non-road to their parcels, everybody had to deal with the negative vibes, like a dark cloud that overcame the general scene, because of the dirty deal itself.

Ironically, John Lingemann was *the* well driller in Santa Cruz, a super well driller, and all his kids were professional well drillers also. So the 160 acres was covered with holes but no water from any of them. There were well drilling machines in the bushes everywhere, all kinds, because his boys had their own well drilling companies. Yet no water for us on the hill.

At the same time, we were all very much into gardening: goats, chickens, horses. We had some really good horses, Arabs, and spent much time training horses and riding.

Los Angeles

Charlie and I were hooked up with The Front Porch Gallery in Venice, California, that later became the Zeneta Kertisz Art Gallery, and so we were doing a lot of art shows and musical performances in Venice and LA. That went on for a long time — somehow living on a remote mountaintop off the grid, and doing art things in a busy modern world which we were not part of, kind of endeared us to a small group of fans.

And then I went to Seven Sanctuaries Gallery, which was run by Carol Cole and her husband John Ernsdorf. She was Nat King Cole's daughter and Natalie's sister, and once upon a time she was Charlie's wife — they were still friends, which gave us a good connection.

It was a very nice gallery in a good location, and I had a successful solo show there, sold a lot of things, and was held over for a month because it got a very good review in the Los Angeles Times. But I decided I had had enough of the big city, and wanted to just spend more time in my studio, and with my family, so I pulled out of LA.

And now Carol has passed and Natalie, her sister, has passed, and Charlie's passed, and Max, and Sharon, Phil, and Gary, and so many others. John and Zeneta Kertisz sold their Venice Gallery, and moved to Ojai. We're still sort of in touch; we're the last of the original Superfabulous Dingulators.

While we were living on The Bump, I began looking for a place for just myself and my family, without the drama, and we finally found it in La Selva Beach. We bought a 10-acre horse ranch at Whiskey Hill Ranch, and raised our seven kids in a modern home that my brother designed for us.

That was a fun time. I had a large 1200-square-foot studio and it was set up to do everything: metal work, stone work, painting, music, anything I wanted to do. I could make noise,

and run heavy equipment. I did a lot of stone carving there.
When the kids grew up, Nancy and I moved to Kauai, because
I was really into surfing and had phased out the horses.

Kauai

We moved to the north shore, Hanalei, and that was fantastic. I
lived my dream, surfing and painting, on Hawaiian time. After
a few years Nancy and I started missing the kids, as they were
all on the mainland, and we were flying back and forth a lot, so
we moved back.

We moved to Wave Avenue in Pismo Beach — a very nice
area on the central coast, but the surf was terrible, and most of
our children and grandchildren were in Santa Cruz, so we moved
back, and we have been living in the Aptos/Seascape area by
the beach ever since.

La Selva Beach

R: And you supported everything all these years with your art?
Pat: Well, I tried to, that was my impossible goal, but I had
a growing family that required a decent cash flow and the art
world is way too flakey, and I am way too lazy when it comes to
outreach and promotion. So between art shows, I ended up doing all kinds of part time work, whatever I could to make money
— anything that was legal, to pay the bills. I mean every kind
of odd job I could get, you know, day laborer, truck driver, all
phases of construction. landscaping, lumberjack, maintenance
man, substitute school custodian, house painter, sign painter,
busboy, waiter, dishwasher, floral designer, horse trainer, art director, mechanic, anything and everything. Nothing too steady,
because I was committed to my art projects. I prefer working
shit jobs in the real world to hanging around art galleries. Plus,
weird work has helped tremendously to shape my art.

When we moved to La Selva Beach, I accidentally and luckily
got a job as custodian for the City of Watsonville, working at
City Hall. I was the head of the night crew that took care of

all the city buildings, and I did that until I was able to retire, which I did at the first opportunity. The people there treated me really well. It worked out perfectly because I had all day to do my artwork, free from outside restrictions and poverty stress; and I could surf and work with my horses, and it provided a steady income.

Also I could practice meditation while working, which I was able to do because of years of zazen practice. I like working meditation more than sitting meditation, so it was exactly the right job for me. I wish I could have done more for the kids, but they have all turned out to be amazing people in spite of the hardships. They are each very exceptional individuals with good lives and bright futures. If the future turns out to be bright.

But anyway, I keep working and doing art. I gave up having shows. I never really think about it, although I have enough artwork to put on several shows at once if forced to. I realized a long time ago that I do not create art for money, or fame, or ego, or to exhibit, to escape, or even for pleasure, although I do enjoy doing it. For me it is simply a personal devotion to self-exploration and revelation through the spontaneous creative processes.

Ralph: Do psychedelics play any role in your story?

Pat: Well, you know, I took a lot of psychedelics back in the day, even before it was illegal. I also ingested some peyote and mescaline, and other things that I can't spell.

When I was young, I was looking for some believable answers to life's mysteries. I tried a lot of different types of substances; luckily I never got hooked on any of them, except maybe herb. I am only hooked on pot like I am hooked on lettuce. I use them and enjoy them both regularly for health reasons, but I can easily do without them if they are not available. You can't say that about heavy drugs like tobacco, booze, coffee, coke, crack, etc. The thing that I have been addicted to most is surfing, because I don't see myself quitting even now in my old age. And acid can be good, because it can take you beyond ego, which can be really a big breakthrough or revelation.

But, you never know what's going to happen once you take it.

It is *not* predictable. I would never promote it. However, I got lucky, and was able to work out a lot of stuff that was hanging me up. Inaccurate attitudes, and certain thoughts about things, so it was good in that respect. The bad thing is that so many good people get burned out and burned up on drugs and alcohol. Addiction is a very tough thing. Acid isn't habit forming, but it can sometimes have negative, damaging effects psychologically.

I hardly smoke at all now — just a couple of puffs in a pipe now and then, usually in the evening. I have a medical pot card, so I am legal, and it helps with anxiety attacks. I haven't smoked tobacco or drunk alcohol in many, many years. When I was younger I had a lot of wild-goose type thoughts and emotions, and the herb seemed to help organize them a little bit, so I could function better. And now, I've had some breakthroughs I guess, and with diet and exercise, and rest and meditation everything seems more unified and flowing.

But I'd say, about LSD — once I took it every day for a month to try to figure out what was going on, and I found the only thing that happened was, it didn't have much effect. But if you only take it once in a while, that's when it's most powerful. People can have very bad trips more often than good ones. It is a very serious substance, a holy sacrament, not to be used as a recreational drug. It is not a shortcut to enlightenment, although it is definitely mind-bending and consciousness-expanding. I'm glad I did all that, but I would not want to do it now.

Ralph: So you're doing meditation and yoga?

Pat: Yeah, I regularly meditate, and do chi gong, yoga, and tai chi. Plus I do a few floor exercises, regular long walks on the beach, and of course surfing.

Compassion

In my everyday life I try to help people who are in need as much as possible, but without going out of my way to look for people who need help. Whenever it comes along, then I'll help. I'm not a person who needs to help people, but I think that philosophically that's a good way to deal with society. Compassion is an important thing. I realize the value in being more compassionate and how it's pretty much opposite to my natural way of actually behaving. So I have to work at it, you know. Like when somebody does something bad to me, my natural human response is to do something even worse to them, and so I've learned not to do that, except in some instances where I might have to prevent them from hurting other people. I try to deal with my own personal rage factor and anger. It's a simple trap to fall into, being really pissed off all the time; it becomes a part of one's personality. Not a healthy thing, because there's so much bad stuff outside of your control. It actually doesn't matter what's outside of your control, you're really only responsible for yourself, and controlling yourself, and when you do that, you pretty much change everything else around and inside you.

I have a lot of desire for everybody to succeed at everything they're doing, unless it is a really dumb, bad, evil thing. And I try to stay out of people's way.

Music

When we performed, Charlie and I only played our creations, and not traditional musical instruments. Part of what we were doing was pushing the envelope. Charlie and I were very much into that and it was very exciting for me.

Eventually, after years of campaigning The Space Bass in galleries and music halls, I didn't want to carry it around anymore, and I couldn't sell it even for a million bucks, which would have been way underpriced, so I just took it to the dump and recycled it. After that, just before we moved to Kauai, I gave almost everything away, all my tools and large paintings and large sculptures.

2. Rick Gladstone

I interviewed Rick in a cafe on February 6, 2016.
The transcript was then transcribed by Becky Luening, and edited by Rick and by Judy Lomba.

Where I'm Coming From & Getting to Santa Cruz

I was born in San Francisco in 1947. When I was seven my
family left the Sunnydale Projects, in Visitacion Valley, on the
south end of the City. and moved down the coast to an old,
dilapidated ranch in the Santa Cruz Mountains, five miles in
from Pescadero. That's where my five sisters and I were raised.
I was seventeen when I graduated from tiny Pescadero High
School, in a class of sixteen students; that's Pescadero and La
Honda kids combined.

My parents decision to make the move was always up for
agonizing reappraisal, but I came to realize that it was influenced
by several things; partly by their idealism: My dad, Joe, was a
merchant marine who had just quit going to sea and had been
in the radical labor movement for a long time; and likewise my
mother, Ann, was a union organizer and part-time secretary for
the painters union — they and their circle of lefties from the
SWP (Socialist Workers Party) were always looking for utopia.

My folks planned the move with another family from our
circle, the idea being an experiment in cooperative living. Joe,
a city boy from Brooklyn, was skeptical, but Ann, as a young
girl, had lived with her family on farms on the east coast and on
state farms in the Soviet Union, and she lobbied hard. So Joe,
miraculously, borrowed fifteen hundred dollars from his father
and with others from our circle we had enough for a down payment on the rundown Stone-Bulstead ranch on Pescadero Creek
Road.

[A coda to my father's borrowed down payment: One of the
characters in the group was Peter Martin. Peter started a poetry
magazine in San Francisco in 1952 and called it *City Lights* (and

he also co-founded the namesake bookstore, with Ferlinghetti, et al.), but by '54 he wanted to move back to New York, so he offered the journal to my dad for fifteen hundred bucks. Joe had to decide: the city lights or the country roads. I sometimes wonder how our life might have otherwise turned out, for better or worse.]

The Ranch

The ranch was eighty-five acres, mostly redwood mountainside, with a ten acre meadow and Pescadero Creek running through it. There were several decrepit wooden cabins on this property, either falling down or molding into the earth under the redwoods, and a long, wooden, barn-like workshop, whose doors were falling off. The Abbotts moved into a lodge-like structure we called the "club house." The spring-fed water system had to be completely restored. All the fences had to be rebuilt to keep in the goats. Our family settled in the lower farmhouse, a ramshackle, drafty, moldy, 14-room structure — with a colony of bats and a giant hive of bees in the attic — that we rehabilitated as best we could. It was an inauspicious beginning.

Concurrent with our move to the country, part of the extended family, the Osbornes, moved from the Candlestick Cove Projects (between Hunters Point and Visitation Valley) to an old Victorian in the Haight-Ashbury. The Haight was a great place in the '50s, a diverse, sleepy neighborhood tucked in between Golden Gate Park and Twin Peaks. But a real cultural sea change had started to build as young artists, students, and blue-collar families, who had been priced out of North Beach, moved in.

We often stayed in the city with our relatives and friends on holidays, usually at the Osborne's — when they weren't coming down to the country. We kids would cruise the Panhandle and Golden Gate Park on bikes, race down Ashbury from Clayton and up Haight St. to Stanyan. We'd go to the Haight Theater (later the "Straight" Theater, a name I detested) in the afternoon, or play basketball at the playground or in the Panhandle until dark. I played little league baseball, with Steve Osborne, for the neighborhood team at Grattan playground off Stanyan Street — there being no such available recreational activity out in the country.

The adults would hang out up on Clayton St., solving the world's problems. Steve's mom, Lily (my Italian mom — my mom was his Jewish mother; they met as socialist youth while in their teens) had been an organizer in the canneries in Monterey. She was a fabulous artist and early innovator of art programs for special-needs kids, and her oldest sister, Mary Fabilli, was a "minor" Beat poet who had been married to another poet — Bill Everson, whom she introduced to Catholicism. He decided to convert and become a monk (maybe marriage can do that to you) and they got an annulment, but I remember Brother Antoninus, in his robe and collar, at dinner on Sundays. Later, Bill, by then re-secularized, came down to teach at UCSC.

Tonia, Steve's older sister, took me to my first political action, in 1962, a sit-in on Auto Row on Van Ness Avenue in San Francisco; and also to my first coffeehouse — the Precarious Vision, which was on Divisadero, I think. Their dad, Selden, one of my father's closest comrades, was a long-time peace activist, longshoreman, and decades-long political foe of Harry Bridges in the ILWU (whose hiring hall was used for the first S.F. Acid Test).

The longshoreman and political philosopher Eric Hoffer (author of *The True Believer*) had become part of the family and would always be at Sunday dinner on Clayton St. Selden had met him during a beef with the Communist Party-leaning ILWU union leadership (like most of our crowd, Selden was a follower of Leon Trotsky and hence in the SWP or one of its splinter groups, and always at war with the CP — supporters of Stalin — over differing visions of the worker's state). Eric became a surrogate grandfather to the Osborne kids and he treated me as a godson. My mom ended up transcribing a couple of his subsequent books directly from his handwritten manuscripts. A self-taught (anti-) intellectual and spellbinding raconteur, he would often come down to the ranch, taking long walks with Steve and me along Pescadero Creek Road, entertaining us with tales of his younger years as a gold-miner and migrant worker.

The grand plan for a communal co-op, a place for all the lefties, as originally conceived, fell through. A summer camp that was supposed to provide income never got off the ground. By 1957, three years into the experiment in cooperative living, Joe borrowed some money and bought out Joan and Charlie, and the Abbotts moved back to Tunnel Road in Berkeley. I recall my father saying that everyone who encouraged our family to make a move to the country found it less romantic when faced with the incredible shit load of work required to maintain a place like that. Nevertheless, the ranch became a gathering spot for many of those who had, up to that point, managed to survive the Great Depression, the Stalinist purges, the Spanish Civil War, World War II and the McCarthy years.

So, because I was raised between San Francisco and Santa Cruz, I got to spend time in both towns, especially since we'd begun to use Santa Cruz — ten miles closer than S.F. — as our nearest "go to" spot for supplies and entertainment. I got to see things play out in a kind of "before, during and after" scenario, in the '50s and '60s. And, although we lived in the country, my family remained part of an urban milieu that included unionists, Marxists and anarchists, as well as bohemians and beats - which were all part of an earlier, pre-hippie counter culture. When my buddies would stop by the ranch and see all the books in our house they knew they weren't in Kansas anymore. By the time I came to live in Santa Cruz in late 1965, I had grown up in virtually two worlds; one as an average country kid, the other in a parallel universe of political and cultural radicals.

By the early '60s, we started to see more and more offbeat characters around — bearded, longhaired or otherwise, loners living in tents or cabins in the hills. The isolation was attractive. Change was in the air.

La Honda

Ken Kesey and his friends — the Pranksters — moved up to La Honda when I was about fifteen. Things got a lot more interesting. We were all curious, and a few of us started checking out the parties at Kesey's before we'd take off for Santa Cruz or Redwood City, looking for kids our own age. During the next year, still just a punk kid, I remember stopping in at Kesey's place a few times with older buddies, sometimes doing a deal or making a score, standing around in the front yard, soaking up the atmosphere. My schoolmate Ray's parents, Mac and Gracie, owned Boots and Saddle Lodge, a restaurant and bar famed for its summer jazz jams and abalone steak dinners. Mac had been a long-time bass player in the S.F. Bay Area, before opening up Boots. Dozens of his old band mates would show up on summer weekends to blow all day and into the evening. Hundreds of people would pour in from the City and the whole town would be jumping.

Boots was literally two hundred feet from Kesey's place, on San Gregorio Road. It was the local bar for the Pranksters. We'd walk around the corner to Ken's pad, past the "no left turn unstoned" sign, across the little bridge into the yard to see if a party was planned for the evening. Further, the bus, was parked off to the side. (I think there is a common misconception that Ken Kesey lived on a "farm" or "ranch" in La Honda. It was actually a fair-sized country-type cabin that sat tucked under some redwoods at the base of a forested hillside, next to the two-lane Highway 84, with a large yard/driveway in front.)

The parties at Kesey's were a whole different ballgame, unlike anything anybody had ever seen. They would often get big and loud, with lots of people, bikers, freaks, wine, beer, weed, acid. Eventually the parties got too frequent, too big and too loud. Everybody knew it would come to a head (no pun intended). There would be scores of parked choppers and cars stretched along the shoulder of HW 84 for a quarter of a mile. The parents of my schoolmates were freaked out, frantically concerned about the virtue of their kids. It was certainly an over-reaction, but predictable. The cops were called multiple times.

The sheriff hated having to make the 70-mile roundtrip over from Redwood City. The Sheriff's Department and the Highway Patrol started impounding bikes, hauling people to jail on various charges, etc. — enough harassment to eventually force the Pranksters to move, some of them to Santa Cruz. But not before I took my first acid trip, with a schoolmate and his sister at their parent's house, a half-mile down the road.

Another strange connection: In 1963, my dad was working over in Palo Alto. His boss, Ray Hennell, was married to Emma, the actual VA nurse on whom the character "Big Nurse" Ratched, in *One Flew Over the Cuckoo's Nest*, was based. They came to visit us at the ranch a few times, and my dad told me they were pretty frosted about the portrayal of Emma in the book and movie, and Ray had confided in him: the hospital was going to sue Kesey for dereliction of duty because he supposedly hid in the closet during his shift as an orderly, working on his story. When I read the novel a couple of years later it felt strange to recall her, standing in the driveway, tight-lipped, in high heels and beehive hairdo, chain-smoking.

Meanwhile, over in Pescadero, in the Butaño off of Cloverdale Road, there was a communal nudist colony, founded by Eric Clough, called Eden West. They were there for several years; I'm not sure exactly how long. I remember a general, uneasy co-existence with the townsfolk, who were civil to Eric and his group and thought of them as slightly lascivious at worst, and best left alone; but, judging from the level of gossip around Williamson's gas station, where I worked for a while, I figured they were more than a little intrigued. Eventually, I'm guessing that due to a combination of increasingly chilly vibes from some Native Sons and Daughters, plus the generally cool summer weather in that part of the canyon, the colony moved to Santa Cruz County in 1963 and settled at 1000 Alba Road, in Ben Lomond.

Bateson

Sometime before Kesey moved to La Honda, he was working at the VA Hospital in Menlo Park and, according to legend, had access to LSD. One of the directors at the VA at that time was Gregory Bateson, and he was interested in the use of LSD for therapeutic purposes, as similar research was being done elsewhere, in Canada and Europe. Gregory and his wife Lois, who were friends of our family, eventually came out to live on the ranch for a couple years.

During the big flood in the winter of '55 (the same one that wiped out downtown Santa Cruz and the old Chinatown — where the Galleria, River Street parking garage, CVS and Trader Joe's are now — our bridge at the ranch washed out, cutting us off from the county road, and it took us two years to rebuild it. In '58, our friends, Jay and Betty Haley and their three young children, rented the clubhouse. Betty, an old political comrade of my parents, was a world-class musician, a concert violinist and pianist. Jay worked with Bateson, who recruited him to join the staff at the Mental Research Institute in Menlo Park, doing some kind of cutting-edge work in psychotherapy along with Milton Erickson, Virginia Satir and others. They were using hypnosis and developing "family therapy" and something called "results therapy", among other things. They started the journal *Family Process*, which Betty edited in the clubhouse. Jay went on to become quite well known in the field of psychology and when the Haleys moved back to Palo Alto to get their kids into better schools, Gregory and Lois moved in.

Greg, formerly married to Margaret Mead, was friendly and right at home in the country, and though a child of the British upper crust, was very informal and down to earth. He would amble down from the clubhouse to our kitchen on Saturday morning, an unfiltered smoke dangling from his lips, shirt half-tucked in, shoes untied and fly open. My mom would laugh and tell him to zip up, pour him a cup of coffee and he would schmooze for a while. I always appreciated it when Greg came in because Joe would get into a conversation with him on some esoteric subject or other, and that would delay going out to start work, which meant I had a reprieve. Plus, I was fascinated by whatever they talked about, including his research with octopi and dolphins. Bateson seemed to enjoy bantering with my dad, who was a very erudite, working-class intellectual. Greg drolly remarked "it's difficult arguing with Marxists and Catholics; they have a system." He had a wealth of knowledge about the flora and fauna, and always invited us to look through his homemade telescope when he set it up on those dark country nights.

A polymath without a PhD, Gregory moved in and out of a succession of fields and disciplines. He said, "You always have to sing for your supper." My mom ended up working for him, preparing transcribed accounts of audiotape therapy sessions. Greg and Lois moved away before their daughter Nora was born, and later he was hired to teach at UCSC, in the late '60s. The Batesons ended up moving in at 1000 Alba Rd., where Eric Clough and the nudist colony had been earlier. They followed on the heels of Ralph Abraham, who had moved out in April, 1974.

Santa Cruz: The Early Years

Living in Pescadero in the late '50s, Santa Cruz was the nearest "big city" (pop. 25,000), forty miles south. We'd go to the boardwalk with visiting relatives and friends, and shop for supplies. Fishing off the wharf with my uncle Lee on occasional Sundays was a special treat. We went to the movies at the Del Mar (I remember seeing "Psycho" there in 1960), or the Rio, and I think there was a theatre on Walnut Street, though it might have been closed by then.

My childhood compadre, John Muñoz, was living in town. His family had moved to Santa Cruz in1961. As young teenagers, in '61 - '62, we used to sneak into the Skyview Drive-In in the trunk of a car or under a blanket on the backseat floor, or we would just hop the fence. Later, when the city morality squad was giving Ron Boise and Peter Demma such a hard time about the statues, I'd shake my head, thinking about the Skyview, because we saw movies there that would soon be considered r-

or x-rated: not hardcore sex but soft porn, with lots of nudity. We pubes couldn't believe our good fortune, that this was right here in our backyard! We were amazed that the owners weren't busted, but we didn't complain.

Mike F. and I would come to Santa Cruz pretty often to hang out with John, and I remember going to the Sticky Wicket (after it had moved from Santa Cruz to the edge of Aptos), a pretty cool coffeehouse. On Saturday nights we would cruise up and down Pacific Avenue. and Beach Street. hoping to meet some girls. We shot pool in the Town Clock Billiards Parlor, located on the first or second block of Front St. on the north end. It was spacious, with low ceilings and lots of atmosphere, a shaded lamp over every table, with an entrance off both Front and Pacific. It was definitely a cool place to hang out and smoke cigarettes, which we could buy at United Cigar, across the street on Pacific. We'd go bowling at Surf Bowl or the Santa Cruz Bowl on Pacific Avenue. In the '70s Randall Kane bought Santa Cruz Bowl, remodeled it, pushed the lanes together to create a dance floor and opened the "New" Catalyst.

Mike and I played ball for Pescadero High against the Catholic Schools around the Monterey Bay. We were, by far, the smallest, as well as the only public school in the league. We played basketball against Holy Cross at the Civic Auditorium and baseball on the big diamond at Harvey West Park, a real treat for us bumpkins. One night, at a basketball game against Palma of Salinas, somebody told the Palma cheerleaders that I was an atheist (I wasn't — I've always been sort of agnostic). After the game they came running over and told me "we're going to pray for your soul." I was flattered, of course, but definitely was more interested in the messengers than the message.

Although very conservative and demographically "older" (third oldest, per capita, in the U.S. in the 1950s), Santa Cruz always had an active sub-culture and youth culture — surfers, for one — and assorted writers and artists around the county, in the hills and by the beaches. This is probably not unusual for beach towns and resort/tourist areas, as creation and recreation share common ground. Capitola was an artist's colony. The Greenwood Lodge, in the hills behind Soquel, was a vacation/summer retreat for families who were associated with the Communist Party. Don McCaslin, from San Jose, and Santa Cruz High alum, Corny Bumpus, played music locally in the '50s and '60s. Heinlein and Hitchcock lived in the area.

With such a spectacular, beautiful, physical setting, accessible to both bay areas, Santa Cruz was a natural destination and gathering spot. But was it necessarily the kind of place where cultural, if maybe not political, revolution might take root?

UC Berkeley

In 1964 I was in my first year at UC Berkeley, studying physics. This was the year of the Free Speech Movement, and I found myself involved with the strikes and picket lines, while still attempting to attend my classes. Remaining in school was paramount, given that I'd soon be eighteen and exposed to the draft if I wasn't enrolled. But the distraction was too much, and I dropped out in my sophomore year.

I worked for nine months for a paving company and then hooked up with my pal Mike on a crew that built state parks. We built two parks in the Santa Cruz area, Sunset Beach State Park on San Andreas Road, and Henry Cowell Park Campground on Graham Hill Road. I decided to stay in town, maybe go back to school. It was a strategy: get a II-S deferment and keep out of Vietnam. I had known, via my parents, about Vietnam since Dien Bien Phu in the middle '50s, and it made me sick and furious that my two best friends were getting sucked into the vortex of war in Southeast Asia. Mike got drafted a year later. John, in the navy reserves, was waiting for his deployment orders. I got my induction notice, refused to go, and began four years of sparring with the draft board in San Mateo.

Our crew had one more park to build, down in Big Sur — Julia Pfeifer Burns State Park — then our work would be finished, as the State had run out of funds for new park construction. While building JPB and living in Big Sur, my crewmates and I heard about a "live-music concert" up in Pescadero, at the

I.D.E.S. Hall. We were flabbergasted, as nobody ever came to Pescadero, let alone to the I.D.E.S. Hall, unless it was in May for the Chamarita, the Portuguese Holy Ghost Festival. Some group was promoting a big bicycle race and they tried to attract more bodies with a rock concert. So we jammed up to Santa Cruz, stopping to pick up my girlfriend Pat and some other friends, and on up to Pesky. We walked into the half-empty hall and I asked someone next to me, "Who are these guys?" "The Warlocks", he shouted as the longhaired, mustachioed keyboardist, Pig Pen, banged down on the first chord. They proceeded to rock the joint like it'd never been rocked before, or since, probably.

SC Communal Pads

I came back up to Santa Cruz from Big Sur and hooked up with John and other old high school friends who had a communal pad over on Avalon Street, off Emeline. This was in late '65, early '66, and so I started living like a Santa Cruz "hippie". We never called ourselves, or thought of ourselves, as hippies. But we were sort of culturally transmuting into what others started calling "hippies." I was pretty skeptical about that kind of labeling.

There were communal pads sprouting up around Santa Cruz. Our place on Avalon St. was a multi-colored, rambling farmhouse. It had high ceilings, large windows and lots of light. A lifeguard friend of ours, Bob Beede, who later taught electronic music and recording at Cabrillo, hooked up a boffo sound system out of parts. We were awash in the great LP's being produced, the S.F. Sound, the British Invasion, FM rock coming on line, Masekela, Handy, Lloyd. Music, as well as any consumables, including food, was always shared. The rent was cheap: for example, I think we were initially paying about $65/mo. for Avalon House, shared by 6-8 people. But that changed over the next couple of years as the expanding university put upward pressure on housing costs.

We had a fluid core of housemates at Avalon St., as did the 7th Ave House, and most of us knew each other from high school.

The 7th Ave. house was a big, old, mid-19th century sea captain's estate, where our good friend Ernie Keller — one of Santa Cruz's Ur-Hipsters- lived, along with some of his former Santa Cruz High classmates. It had lots of exotic trees planted around the grounds, of which only the stately cork-oak tree remains, standing gallantly in front of the gas mart on the corner of 7th and Soquel Ave. Local artist Jimmy Phillips — who created one of the iconic posters of the '60s, "The Next Supper" — had painted a giant portrait of Braunstein, the Zig-Zag man, on the fireplace, and Ernie had hooked up speakers and muted colored lights in all the rooms, put rugs and pillows on the floors, and there was amazing music always playing — a great place to trip. Other communal places I remember include Stone Hill, and, a bit later, Camp Joy up in the San Lorenzo Valley.

Some real interesting things occurred at Avalon Street. Ed Leslie, a local real estate mogul, came by the house one day in a big, red Cadillac convertible, looking for our housemate, Eddie Lawrence, who did odd-jobs for him. Short-haired, wearing shades and dressed in informal business attire, Ed stood out like a sore thumb and looked like a narc, but was friendly enough. Eddie had invited him to come over for dinner. After we ate, he said he wanted to try smoking some grass, so a joint was rolled; he took a few puffs and settled back to listen to some Beatles on the turntable. He must have had a good time because he started coming around quite often, his hair started growing down over his collar, he traded his leather shoes for sandals, and switched to groovier threads. Subsequently he began to promote rock concerts and started managing a local band named Snail, and for the next several years they had a heck of a run.

Howard Dumble used to come by fairly often and have dinner with us. He was one of the earliest in a line of very talented musicians, DJs and music-makers from Bakersfield who migrated to Santa Cruz in the '60s and '70s, including Cindy Odum and Michael Tanner. Howard was a fine guitar player but an even better electronics engineer and his custom amps are legendary in the halls of Rock 'n Roll. He'd plug in his latest creation and proceed to tear it up for a couple of hours.

Our pad was a popular spot and we had lots of jams and parties, and we always had food to share. It was a gathering place for many local friends (the sons and daughters of City Fathers and Mothers and local Chamber of Commerce types) whose names I'll withhold as a personal courtesy, with one exception: our dear friend, Mike Fox, who succumbed to an incurable disease at the age of twenty-three. His father, who owned Fox Medical Supply on Ocean St., donated money to the city to create a park, next to the Riverside Bridge, in Mike's memory, which still serves the public well to this day.

Here, like everywhere, I suppose, people were in motion, looking for roots, coming and going, crashing for a while, moving on, jamming up to the Haight or Golden Gate Park to catch the free concerts, traveling to New Mexico, Northern California, Europe, the far east, Latin America, wherever. It was a time when some folks were digging in and others were letting go; some taking off, some landing; some looking for place and some looking for space. A stream of European hipsters, traveling around, flowed through Avalon House, kids from Spain, France, Denmark, Sweden, England. A whole crowd of Persian hippies, all "related to the Shah" but dodging the Iranian draft, frequently partied at Avalon St.

We were experimenting. Everyone started eating lots of brown rice and cooking in the style of George Ohsawa's macrobiotic diet, trying to avoid becoming sanpaku. We started our own ad-hoc collectivization of the food scene: one of our family, Jean Claude, discovered all the "bruised" but usable vegetables that were being tossed out at Albertson's Market so we started "dumpster diving" and bringing home boxes of carrots and celery, onions, beets, etc. and cooking them up in big pots on our stove. We called it "Albertson's Stew", and distributed it around to several pads — we did this a couple of times a week. We learned that Maddox's Bakery in Soquel tossed out their day-old loaves before they went to bake, at four in the morning, so we'd swing by after two a.m. or so, in the back parking lot and would just ask if we could take it, a win-win situation. They were pleased and we'd drive off with two or three gunnysacks full of wheat, rye, sourdough loaves, rolls, and breadsticks. As with the stew, we distributed. We identified a couple of restaurants, like Luther's on Seabright, who would give us their "remainder" soup if we came by around midnight. We would end up with two or three gallons worth: then we'd make the rounds of hip pads.

Later, when our pad scene moved to Blain St., we installed a large vegetable garden and traded avocados (collected mostly from the giant tree in our backyard) at Pacific Grain and Grocery on Pacific Avenue for bulk grain, rice and oil; we located owners of vacant lots and got permission to grow corn. At one time we had three or four lots, at least a quarter-acre or more, in production, and we routinely culled mussels from beaches north of town.

Another food-related note: Right after the landlord booted us out of Avalon House in '67, Eddie Lawrence saw a classified ad in the Sentinel about a bakery going out of business in Boulder Creek. Eddie was compulsive and right away he wanted to go buy the equipment they were selling for dimes on the dollar. I couldn't talk him out of it because he "always dreamed of being a baker", so, with the understanding that I'd only help move and set up the stuff, we drove our bus up to Boulder Creek, bought some big mixers, an oven and some smaller baking tools, and installed it in a little storefront Eddie had located in the little alley facing the back of what's now the Seabright Brewery. We named it the Trinity Bakery and Eddie immediately set to baking crunchy wheat bread; but, predictably, in six months he grew bored with the project and decided to sell. Two fellows, Gary and Richard, who were starting an organic bakery named Staff of Life showed up with cash to buy Eddie out and I was happy that the equipment found a good home. And a few years after that, Ed Leslie and Eddie teamed up again and opened Recycled Lumber on 38th Ave.

People and Places

I first met Peter Demma at the Hip Pocket, in, I think, 1965. Peter was hosting a discussion group one night a week in the back room of the bookstore. I remember that you could get to the back room without going through the book store by coming in from Front St., through the Carriage Room of the St. George (before the Old Catalyst was there), down a narrow hallway that later became part of the bar. I thought it was pretty cool of Peter to offer a gathering place, and was encouraged by the possibilities of the local scene. I got to know Peter a lot better some years later when we were next-door neighbors in the River Flats, on Campbell Street. He was a pretty intense guy, funny, with a sharp gleam in his eye, real radical and into some pretty wild stuff

For about a year, in 1966, myself, John M., Bob Anderson and a couple of others in our circle hung out and drank beer at Van's Village in Capitola, owned by a very hip guy named Sonny. It had, hands down, the best jazz juke box in the Monterey Bay Area. It was later purchased by Tom Louagie and rechristened The Local, in a "name that pub" contest.

We went up to Boulder Creek to outdoor jams at Max Hartstein's in the summertime, and played flutes and drums. I went a couple of times but Bob was a regular.

My girlfriend Pat and I started going up to the Barn when word got around that you could party up there, though we all thought, "Seriously, in Scotts Valley?" We went to an open house where people were invited to help paint the inside of the Barn. I think that was the first time I remember seeing Leon Tabory and Joe Lysowski. We went to hear music quite often: New Delhi River Band, Country Joe, and others I'm forgetting. I didn't meet Joe Lysowski until a few months later at Peter Demma's house in Santa Cruz — though I might be getting my dates mixed up. I was with Bob A., who was doing a little business deal with Peter, and Joe was there. Peter was getting ready to go on a road trip to the Deep South and Joe had painted Peter's VW Bug all colorful and psychedelic. I remember Bob, incredulous, asking "you're gonna go through the south in that?"

but Peter assured us it was cool and pointed out the "Support Your Local Police" sticker he'd slapped on the bumper (or back hood). When he got back he told me he never once got stopped. As for Leon Tabory, I remember meeting him a couple of times, briefly, once at his place (I think) out in the La Selva Beach area (a vague and possibly false memory).

About that Scotts Valley thing: In 19i66 I helped my pal, D.J. Carlisle, with a production of Michael McClure's *The Beard*, which he directed. I had met Carlisle, a Watsonville High grad, in the Cabrillo College Theatre department, a nationally re-garded program run by Dolores Abrams, whose family owned Abrams Department Store on Pacific Avenue. Dolores was Broadway-trained and dedicated, and D.J. was one of her protégés, a tal-ented actor, writer and artist. But for some reason the venue he lined up for the premier was the community center in Scotts Valley. If you have never seen *The Beard*, it's a real powerful comment on American Culture. There are only two characters — Billy The Kid and Jean Harlow. There's a lot of sexual ten-sion and raw emotion, and they engage in oral sex at the front of the stage. At the dress rehearsal on Thursday we got booted out of town and ended up at the Unitarian Church on Freedom Blvd.

One day, sometime in '66, Eddie Lawrence and our friend Cage drove down to Brownsville, Texas and came back with about 5000 peyote buttons. The town practically levitated for the next few weeks. I took the opportunity to engage in some serious questing and piano playing on the funky upright in the living room at Avalon, and to take in a Giants night game at Candlestick Park. I was stupefied by the intense green of the outfield. To this day I swear I saw Willie Mays flap his arms, swoop into the air and catch a ball in his mouth.

People were starting to home-grow reef so the quality of the available supply improved, if you could afford it. But, with a big government push to criminalize the good drugs, the bad shit took over. In the next couple of years, the drug scene changed, not as quickly or dramatically as in the Haight, which by the fall of '67 was already ugly and mean. I had moved up to S.F.

in late '67 and it was dangerous to be on Haight Street. The real "Summer of Love" was '66, not '67 as the media would have it. We weren't immune in Santa Cruz though, and it got mean and ugly in its own way right here in River City. People started shooting at hippies up in the San Lorenzo Valley.

One night, on my twenty-first birthday, I was living in S.F. and visiting friends in Santa Cruz, down in the little cottage apartments facing the bay at the end of Seabright Ave. After a swell evening of food, drink, and smoke, I came out the front door feeling mellow and got into my old Falcon pick-up, and decided to head down to the Catalyst for a birthday nightcap. As I started the engine a vehicle behind me turned on its lights. I took off to turn up Seabright and the car rushed up and cut me off, forcing me to the curb. There were literally six young guys, in tee shirts and short hair (mine was not short). I stared at them, stunned, as the front passenger window rolled down, and the nearest dude started screaming at me "you motherfuckin' hippie, we're gonna kill you if you don't get outta town", and then they all started yelling at once. They looked like a pack of mad dogs, snarling and frothing at the mouth. I wasn't sure if I was hallucinating but I could tell I was starting to hyperventilate. I tried to clear my head and process the events. I kept my window rolled up but when the guy in the drivers-side back seat opened his door to get out I gunned my engine, rode up on the curb and slid in front of their car and raced up the street. They took off in hot pursuit and I hit the light on Murray, making a hard left, continuing toward the trestle and down past Riverside to Laurel. They stayed right behind me as I accelerated up Laurel, miraculously hitting green lights, barreled right on to Center, and, still unable to shake them, sped up toward City Hall, careened around the corner on Locust and screeched to a halt in front of the City Police Department. My pursuers came up slowly and stopped a short distance behind, sat there for a moment, then wheeled around me and sped away. There were a couple of police cars parked in front but no cops in sight. My adrenaline rush slowly started to subside and I sat there, dazed, trying to reflect on what had just happened, my thoughts in a jumble. "Right here in Santa Cruz?" I thought. "Are you kidding me?" Another couple of minutes later I drove over to the Catalyst and parked in the County Bank parking lot across Front St., got out and walked into the bar just before last call, and feeling only marginally calmer, ordered my first legal beer.

It all seemed to culminate a couple of years later, at the end of the decade, with the media triumphantly anointing us as the "Murder Capital of the World". I was publishing the local "underground" newspaper at the time, and calls were pouring in to the Sentinel from all over, everyone wanting the grisly, juicy details, and the city editor at the Sentinel was merrily giving everybody our phone number. His attitude seemed to be, "ask the hippies, it's their deal." If nothing else, it sure as hell was the end of innocence.

A (non) apocryphal tale — something I recall but can't document (partly because I refuse to subscribe to the on-line Sentinel in order to gain access to the archives): through the late '50s and early '60s, during spring break, the local beaches and Boardwalk were drawing bigger and bigger crowds of partying high school and college kids, with lots of alcohol being consumed. Year by year it got rowdier and rowdier until a riot broke out on the beach at the Boardwalk during spring break in '66. Law enforcement from all over the area was summoned and something like 450 arrests were made for assault, battery, drunkenness, resisting arrest and general mayhem. The city council was aghast, consternation all around. What to do? They decided to outlaw alcohol on the beach, a ban enforced to this day. But I happened to notice an editorial in the Sentinel at the end of spring break in '67, complaining bitterly about "'clouds of smoke and the smell of marijuana wafting above the Boardwalk." Which goes to show you can't please everybody: the number of arrests that year? One.

The Catalyst

The Catalyst opened in April of '66, in the back of the St. George Hotel. It was a originally a co-op, backed by some local professors and liberal professionals: philosophy professor, Sam Bloom; Norm Lezin (owner of the Tannery); Ann Reed; Stan Stevens (Stan was a founder of the local chapter of the A.C.L.U., in 1961), and others I can't remember. And its mission, roughly, was to be a gathering place, in the spirit of community togetherness, and, perhaps, to forge and foster lines of communication between the town and the university.

Al and Patti DiLudovico managed the Catalyst in the spirit of its name: a community gathering place, and it quickly became a de facto public living room and hiring hall for the local hip scene. My buddy, Lex van Zyl, was the first bouncer, and worked the deli counter. (Technically, the first bouncer, as Lex reminds me, was our pal Jesse, a sturdy, but sweet-tempered black guy from East St. Louis, who lasted about one day and quit, deciding shoe repair and drinking beer was more his speed.) From a good cup of coffee for a reasonable price to a decent deli sandwich and a no "minimum purchase" policy, one could spend the better part of a day hanging out, reading, shooting the breeze with Bob Hall or his brother Charlie, playing chess, or lining up work, all in the aged splendor of the old Carriage Room. Most of the construction work and odd jobs that kept me alive in those years were secured there, and later, in the early '70s, I played many gigs at the Catalyst — perhaps as many as forty — with the band Jango.

The colorful, neo-Byzantine paint job on the brick façade facing Front St. was the creation of our good friend Steve Desmond, in the late '60s. As I recall, he worked mainly for free food and drink. Acoustic acts performed during the week. I remember wandering in one Wednesday night and catching a longhaired guy strumming an acoustic guitar and singing real smooth. Between sets I asked him his name and where he was from. He said "I'm Pat Simmons. I hitchhiked over from San Jose." I came back to hear him a couple more times before he disappeared and resurfaced playing with the Doobie Brothers.

When Randall Kane bought the place, in the late '60s, it definitely changed. It was still mellow in the daytime but soon became a full-on nightclub in the evening. Randall built a bar, where he and his cohort could hang out and drink beer. He commissioned the great local portrait artist, Kitty Wallis, to do a huge oil painting, fit for a boys club, and paid my dear friend Danni Long to pose for it, nude, on a white bear rug, and he hung it over the bar. The same painting still hangs, I believe, over the bar in the "new" Catalyst. (Danni's husband at the time, Richard Long, did horoscopes and charts and told me mine indicated I would have a tough life. Maybe he was right, but I guess it depends on what you mean by "tough.")

Our extended circle had a tradition of going to the Catalyst on Saturday morning for breakfast, one that started in the old Cat and continued on in the new. Families grew over time as babies were born and finally, unable to bear the commotion, Randall 86'd the lot of us, thereby punching our ticket into a pretty cool club.

The "back-bar" in the old Cat was built by a buddy, Stan Fullerton, a part Native-American, larger-than-life, pipe-puffing, beer-chugging, pastrami-chompin' character. An artist and sculptor, he told me he had been an orphan and grew up on a reservation in Oregon, and that he had lived in North Beach in the late '50s and knew a lot of the Beats. He built the back-bar for free, with the understanding from Randall that he could tend bar. I bring this up because, though this occurred just outside the pre-'68 scope of these recollections, there's an interesting connection: several of my mates and I worked for Stan in the late '60s, during the "coast barn wood" craze, when the weathered, silver, redwood-siding of deteriorating coastside barns was being bought up for ridiculous sums of money by interior decorators to satiate a torrid fad. Every lawyer, mortgage broker, and tax accountant had to have their office paneled with coast barn wood. We would buy these dilapidated structures — the ones you see when you're driving up the coast and say "oh, look at that quaint old barn, ready to fall over" — from local farmers, carefully disassemble the structures, and haul them away on Stan's beautifully restored '36 Diamond T flatbed. We extended this work to any old buildings being removed or torn down around town and scratched out an existence in the recycled wood business.

So, finally, here's the connection: Stan eventually married the slender, intellectual, Professor Gail Jackson Putney, sometime in the late '60s, an unlikely pairing that endured, and, as Gail Fullerton, she became the first female president of San Jose State University (she recently passed away). Before that she had been married to a noted sociology professor and environmentalist, Snell Putney. When she divorced Snell, in the mid-'60s, he took to living on his boat in the Santa Cruz Yacht Harbor, and he parked his restored '30s Packard in the harbor parking lot. When Tom Scribner and a few others and myself started the Redwood Ripsaw in '67 we took a staff photo, and used Snell's car for the photo shoot.

Tom Scribner and the Redwood Ripsaw

The earliest photo of me in the family archives — at four months old — shows me lying naked on a blanket, in the backyard of a little farm house on El Dorado Ave., out in rural Live Oak. There were still a lot of farms and orchards out there between sleepy Santa Cruz and sleepier Capitola, right up into the sixties. The property belonged to an old friend of my parents from the radical labor movement, Herman Bollman. Recently retired from house painting and union organizing in San Francisco, he remarried and bought this little farm, and my folks, when they could persuade someone with a car to make the 160-mile round trip all the way down bumpy, windy Highway 1, (2 lanes all the way) would come to visit Herman. Years later, in 1966, I would run into Herman (by then in his '80s) from time to time in the Old Catalyst, as his wife had kicked him out and he was living in the St. George Hotel.

Meanwhile, I spent many an afternoon in the early "old" Catalyst, a good deal of it drinking coffee, kibitzing and hatching revolutionary scenarios with Tom, so these encounters with Herman would occasionally occur while Tom and I were schmoozing, and would invariably reinforce my general antipathy toward the endless, Byzantine disputes of leftist sectarianism: Tom, as most

locals know, was an ex-Wobbly and later a member of the CP —
the Communist Party of the U.S.A., founded by supporters of
Joe Stalin and the Soviet Union. My family's background was
with the CP's bitter rival, the SWP. — the Socialist Workers
Party — which supported Leon Trotsky and his version of the
worker's state. I never bugged Tom about his CP past and he
never hassled me about Trotsky, but whenever Bollman, an old
SWP/Socialist Party member, would walk by, Tom, who was
usually quite garrulous, would clam up. Herman would stop at
our table, say hello to me and look at Tom: "Herman", Tom
would grunt and Herman, stone-faced, would nod and mutter
"Tom", and walk away.

Tom had retired from 50+ years of working in the woods
and mills in Louisiana and the Northwest (and probably Minnesota, where he was born), most recently as a pond monkey
in Humboldt County, and was living in Davenport with his second wife, Mary, in 1964. He continued to write and self-publish,
typing hunt-and-peck — he had only 2 fingers on his left hand,
not uncommon for a woodsman. He started losing digits as a
teenager, in sawmills; consequently, being a self-taught musician, he switched from the fiddle to the saw. He suffered some
other gruesome injuries over the years, the details of which you
can find in his collection of writings, *Lumberjack*, and newspaper, *Lumberjack News*.

His life and political views are pretty well documented so
you can look them up if you're interested, but a couple of basics:
wherever he had lived and worked he agitated for socialism and
industrial unionism. He joined the IWW in 1914, when he was
16, and hung with them until 1925, when, as he used to say, "I no
longer could find anyone to pay my dues to." He then joined the
fledgling American Communist Party and remained loyal until
he couldn't stand it anymore and quit the Party in the mid-
fifties, though he continued to write and speak out against the
capitalist system. He loved being a gadfly and had the *Maoist
People's Daily, English Edition*, delivered to his post office box
in Davenport. He giggled and assured me, "that sure got that
nosey postmaster's lips ta flappin'." Then he and Mary moved

to Santa Cruz in '65 or early '66. I met Tom when I first came to town and we remained close friends for the rest of his life.

In 1967 Tom wanted to crank up the mimeograph one more time and we hatched a plot, over coffee in the Catalyst, to do a newspaper — more of a political broadside — to rail against the Vietnam war, and generally raise some hell. As hip as the Catalyst was, Tom would say, "this place is a hotbed of middle-of-the-road extremism." Tom called a meeting at his and Mary's house on Kaye St. in Beach Flats, and John Sanchez, John Tuck, Carol Staudacher, Al Johnson, Dr. Paul Lee and myself (there might have been one or two others) showed up and we hammered out the basics. Once we got going we decided to use the photo-offset process so it would look like a real tabloid-style newspaper. Of course, that was more costly and our ad base in those years was pretty slim: Manuel's Restaurant, Al Johnson's Pottery Studio and Ellen's Custom Earrings. Tom, John S., John T. and myself did most of the work and writing. Paul Lee also wrote a couple of pieces. The whole enterprise lasted about eight issues.

The Experience of Politics

I had learned pretty quickly that I always seemed a little too political for my "'hippie'" mates and a little to "hip" for the politicos, which suited me perfectly. The availability of pretty good acid, peyote, mescaline, and a lot of crappy weed was not lost on me, but I was looking for political action.

In 1966 I had enrolled at Cabrillo and was an "unaffiliated" member of the SDS Northern California Regional Steering Committee and wanted to stir up some activity. A year before, in '64-'65, some local kids, Sandy I. and Doug R., had attempted to start a chapter of SDS but had dropped out of school. Myself, and a couple of others, including Lex van Zyl, Pat Dooling, and Kevin Callahan began to distribute anti-war, draft resistance and civil rights literature. It was not easy dealing with the administration. One time we got Manny Chavez, Caesar's brother, to come speak on campus about La Huelga and the

UFW. When Manny arrived, around five pm, we all went to the room we'd secured and found we were locked out. We couldn't get anyone to open it for us. So we went over to Manuel's in Seacliff Beach and Manny Santana let us have our meeting in the restaurant, with free beer and chips, and then he fed Manny C. and a couple of us student organizers "on the house."

On the other hand, I landed a part-time job as administrative assistant to Bill Grant, head of the English Department at Cabrillo. I continued to agitate on campus, trying to generate some political dialogue, a real grind at a commuter campus. Bill wasn't very political but didn't mind as long as I got my work done. We had some limited success, promoting debates on the war, setting up draft counseling, collecting food and clothing for the UFW, which Lex van Zyl, John M. and I took down to Delano. There were some very hip teachers at Cabrillo, including Fred Levy, Pat Mahoney, Dolores Abrams, Pete Varcados, and Peter Fahrquar, and others who had just joined the faculty, like Sandy Lydon and Kirby Wilkens. Before I left, in '67, I recall Bill reviewing resumes on some cool folks that he subsequently hired, including T. Mike Walker and Mort Marcus (though on that point I'm not sure).

In the summer and fall of '66 I worked on Richard Miller's congressional campaign. Dick was running for the Democratic nomination against Fred Farr, Sam's father, and was part of an anti-Vietnam war slate that included independently wealthy Phil Drath in Marin County, Ed Keating of Palo Alto (publisher of *Ramparts Magazine)* and Robert Scheer (editor of *Ramparts*) in Berkeley. Ours was the only campaign without any money, as Dick was a three-days-a-week professor of history at the San Francisco Art Institute, commuting from Pacific Grove and running a shoestring operation. Politically independent, wild-haired and bearded, he was a witty, fiery orator ("The only ism I believe in is metabolism"), at times difficult to understand because he had a split lip, but he always got his point across. Drath had fundraisers with the likes of Joan Baez and the Dead, so somebody who knew somebody helped us contact the Jefferson Airplane and they came down to do a benefit for us at the Civic

Auditorium. It was a great, swirling night of music, that attracted about five hundred folks and we came out ahead after expenses.

Our strategy was to make sure we held a lead in liberal-leaning Watsonville, broke even in evenly divided Monterey, and focused on Republican Santa Cruz, which didn't yet have the liberal bloc-vote of UCSC that later would come to dominate local politics. What few bucks we had went into canvassing on the north end of Monterey Bay, and it almost worked: we split in Monterey, won Watsonville by a couple of hundred, but lost Santa Cruz by four hundred. Even so, despite the odds, Richard ended up garnering the greatest percentage of the democratic vote of all the anti-war candidates — a hollow if not moral victory.

Through political activity in the Peace and Freedom Party and the California for a New Politics campaign, I met many political activists in town, including: Alice and Manny Santana, John and Sherry Tuck, Paul Dragavon; Flo and John Sanchez; Burt and Lois Muhly; Dan and Pat Miller; Carol Staudacher; Bill and Edith Weintraub; Al and Clarice Johnson; Jim and Jeanne Houston; Sam and Ethel Bloom; Carlie and Stan Stevens; Paul Lee; Tom Scribner; the King sisters; Jim and Katy Heth; Sandy and Alan Lowe; Lou Harrison, and many others I'm forgetting.

By mid '67 I was going up to the Bay Area more frequently, to demonstrations and rallies. I took a carload of friends up to Stop the Draft Week, a massive street action that lasted several days. Things were starting to escalate. And the establishment was beginning to push back, real hard.

The City on the Hill in the Town

The University was definitely influencing the cultural and political landscape of Santa Cruz, and would do so to a greater extent over the ensuing decades. World-class scholars and whip-smart students were flowing into town. Though the campus, cast in Ivory Tower terms, was thought of as a "City on the Hill," its influence was spilling over into the community in many ways. For one thing, it provided employment opportunities and jobs for the local citizens, which, besides the tourist industry, had been sorely lacking. Campus voters reshaped the community's political profile. Tug-of-war battles began to wax and wane between the university and the community over land use, infrastructure costs, housing pressure, tax base and institutional hegemony.

Many students and faculty brought to the table a sharp critique of the capitalist system and the war, and the University's role in supporting imperialism. Pioneering work was ramping up in many disciplines and barriers were being breached. Political activism was the new normal. Use of mind expanding, if not altering, substances put UCSC near the top of the class nationally. In fact, according to my daughter, who attended tiny Hampshire College in Massachusetts (also started in the mid-sixties, and part of the Amherst five-college consortium), UCSC, to this day, is the second choice of more students at her school than any other college, precisely because of its interdisciplinary slant and the availability of good reef. And all this, on balance, contributed to the general expansion of local "consciousness." I mean, heck, up there they even study its history.

I used the campus facilities shamelessly, mainly the east field house for basketball (after the first year that is; during the year of the trailers, I seem to remember, it was used as a dining hall). I also frequented McHenry Library four or five times a week, as a sanctuary: a quiet place to read; access to all the journals; use of the listening rooms. I figured, "Why not, I'm a taxpayer." The cultural events were a huge addition to the local scene and I attended many lectures, concerts, dance and art shows over the years. I once sat five feet away from Chet Baker, in a pretty small room, at, I think, Merrill College, as he jammed with some local cats. Chet kept snapping at one of the players for missing the "one" every time the head came around.

[There is a kind of interesting story concerning McHenry - not the library but the chancellor. Selden Osborne, our old comrade, who had retired from the waterfront and would soon be walking across the United States with a group of peace activists, periodically hitchhiked down to Santa Cruz (his jalopies were always in various states of disrepair) and I would meet him at the Catalyst. He had a cousin living here, whom I only slightly knew, but his real motivation was to go up to the UCSC campus and visit with Dean McHenry, who, as it turned out, had been a classmate of his at Stanford. Selden had a BA from Stanford in the '30s and an MA in political philosophy from UC Berkeley, but had chosen the life of a blue-collar worker in order to organize unions and further the revolution. They made an odd duo, Selden and Dean, but there's an even stranger twist: they were not only classmates, but also housemates at the rooming house that Selden's mom ran, as a single parent, in Palo Alto. And for four years, Selden and Dean had only two other housemates: Clark Kerr, future president of the UC system, and Frank Murphy, future chancellor of UCLA. So, while Selden spent his life trying to enlighten and lead the working class, the other three were busy educating the bourgeoisie.]

Postscript, 1969: *The Free Spaghetti Dinner*

I came back to town after a year and a half in San Francisco and Berkeley. Things were pretty hot in Berserkland, metaphorically speaking, in the early spring of '69. Some members of our affinity group went to chill up at communes in Mendocino. One couple, Steve and Pat, followed me down here and were hanging out briefly at John M.'s cabin off Branciforte. Another couple, close friends of mine and part of the UATWMF collective back east, stayed with us a few days and then jammed up to Black Bear.

After a month, Steve, Pat, another buddy, Chuck Garner (a genuine sage-brush philosopher, born in Muskogee, Oklahoma) and I went looking for a house and located a vacant Victorian on Blaine Street, right behind where the "new" county jail now stands. A spacious farm house, it was perfect for a communal set-up, so we went to the County Building right across Water St., found out the county had taken it over, and we rented it for 150/mo. — a great deal. Several folks moved in, including some of the old Avalon gang. John M. moved into one half of an old wooden garage on the edge of the property, and he and Jean Claude built a dark room in the other half. We de-weeded an approximately forty-by-forty foot patch and installed a big garden, hooked up with our local pals The Barn Brothers — Don Tabor and Paul Kohlman (boat builders and cabinet makers who had grown up in Ben Lomond and had one of the large barns at the Sash Mill as their workshop), and combined both locations into one real functional, productive "family."

I was itching to do another paper, in line with the other "Alternative Press" journals that were cropping up all over the country — from the pioneering days of *The Berkeley Barb, The Oracle, The East Village Other, The White Panther* from Detroit, etc. Steve, who was trying to get into grad school at UCSC, and Pat, were game, so we called a meeting at Blaine St., attended by several housemates (I'm not sure about this list) including: John M., Chuck G., Souxie C., Steve (Said) and Pat D. and some other interested folks like T. Waldo Buck and Diane G., and others I unfortunately can't remember. We cooked up a big pot of spaghetti and that inspired the paper's name. We wanted to use the motto, "all the news that's fit to eat" and print it on rice paper with vegetable-dye ink, but that proved to be financially unrealistic. Steve and I secured a business license, we built a layout table in the basement and we were off and running. The first issue came out in November (I think) of 1969, with a cover-photo montage created by John M. that showed Supervisor Henry Mello of Watsonville, on the steps of the brand new County Courthouse, addressing a huge crowd at an anti-Vietnam war rally.

The paper had a political/environmental/community slant, with great graphics by T. Waldo and other talented artists who joined our staff over the next several months. Everyone worked volunteer and it was a real dedicated crew. We tried selling it for thirteen cents a copy, trying to stay editorially independent of advertisers, but gave up real quick. Giving it away free and developing a display-ad base to pay the bills worked out ok as, by then, there was a pretty large group of hip merchants and craftspeople around, enough to support the basic overhead/costs of putting out the paper. After a couple of issues we moved to a two-office suite on Pacific Ave., on the second floor of the wooden building (whose name I've forgotten) across from the old County Courthouse (later to become the Cooper House). We were in between the Musicians Union office and the Monterey Bay regional office of the *San Jose Mercury*. We could look out on to Pacific Avenue and we worked all day and night. Soon, we took on a business manager, Cash Sales, who hustled display ads for a percentage. His partner, Carole, an RN, joined the staff, and eventually became one of the first Santa Cruz midwives and founders of the Birth Center.

The FSD ramped up to a 32+ page bi-weekly and evolved into a uniquely Santa Cruzy periodical, and, though it took a little while, we got mostly positive feedback from the community, from advertisers, and at "Underground Press" conferences. I wrote an editorial, in the form of a poem, for the second issue, attempting to state our "mission." I worried that it was a bit over-the-top but Steve, who was still trying to line up his graduate studies, and was in contact with some of his former professors at UCB (Sheldon Wolin, Norm Jacobson and John Schaar — who would soon be coming to UCSC to teach) — ran into Norman O. Brown, who told him he liked the poem. I felt relieved. Ralph Abraham, whom I knew from rapping over coffee in the Catalyst, wrote a column. We did some real good stuff, both new-agey and politically radical — but not everybody was convinced. A certain dour, local bookstore owner assured us we were "juvenile" and the paper was "fish wrap."

We emphasized an ecological perspective with an anarchist slant, when most folks were wondering, "what's ecology?" We offered community groups two pages of space to create copy and lay out their ideas and programs, which led to issues with full two-page spreads by: a local Fullerian collective, on constructing geodesic domes; a spread by Max Hartstein on the 25th-Century Ensemble; a description of programs at the Community School; a heads-up on PG&E's plans for a local nuclear power plant — pretty much what a hipster would expect or want from a Santa Cruz periodical: sort of the anti-Sentinel. In fact, sometime in

the first few months we did a big smack-down of the Sentinel.
Dylanologist Steve Pickering joined the staff and did his thing.
We created and published the program and guide to, and com-
mentary on, the first Earth Day in Santa Cruz — April, 1970.
The paper was available around the Monterey Bay and had a
distribution of over 15,000, and spawned — in the words of our
dear friend and staff member, Mischa Adams — "a whole chain
of begats" which was chronicled in a retrospective by the *Metro*
(before it was swallowed up by the *Good Times*). After two years
I sold the "business" to our graphics staff: Anders Paul; Kentus
Americus (creator of the great '60s poster "The World"); and
Bill Buritta, for thirty-two dollars and fifty cents, what the original license cost me. They changed the name to *Sundaz* — and
I contributed articles for a couple more issues. I never made a
dime but had a helluva good time.

I definitely should also acknowledge the *Black Mountain Press*,
a literary and local community journal that was part of the scene
here in the early to mid-sixties; and also, the *Balloon Newspaper*,
a cartoon/art format publication that was around from the late
60's on. Stellar artists like Futzie Nutzle, Henry Humble and
Spinny Walker turned out some great stuff, and we included
their work as an insert in some issues of the FSD.

Part II

The 25th Century
Ensemble, 1964

3. Max Hartstein

Several writings (including two entire books) by Max were posted on our website, *The Hip Santa Cruz History Project*, from October, 2002, though August, 2005. He passed away August 8, 2011, at age 82. These were combined and edited by Judy Lomba for this volume.

I had a wonderful new relationship developing with my friend, Sharon. We decided to move to Marfil, in Mexico, where I had a studio. We brought her young son, Lee, with us and settled in as a family. But after six months in Marfil, Sharon's and my relationship began to cool down. We discussed taking a sabbatical from each other for a few months. She wanted to live in Santa Cruz and I would, after making sure she and Lee were set up in a comfortable home, return to Mexico. We still got along, there were no quarrels, it was very civilized. We intended the separation to be only temporary. The idea was to rekindle the flame. We drove back to Santa Cruz and found a charming cottage just across the street from the ocean. You could hear the surf from the bedroom. It was idyllic, lots of windows and some very attractive neighbors – a young couple and their three babies each a year apart.

We got acquainted immediately. Their names were Pat and Nancy Bisconti. He was a surfer, an artist, a poet, a humorist, and a philosopher. She was an artist, a poet, a calm and caring mother, and a woman who could make do with very few resources. He was a handsome, lean, and surfing sculpted Italian American. He drove a brightly painted Hudson. It was completely covered with his artwork and philosophical sayings such as, "Faster to the Disaster!" There was a chuckle on every fender; the car was a real work of art.

Nancy was of English heritage. She was small, petite, good natured, and beautiful with long straight dark brown hair. She was of a more serious nature, more mature than her years, and deeply dedicated to her role as wife and mother. Her love and appreciation of Pat was an inspiration. They lived in a beach house cottage next to Sharon's. We all smoked pot and got along famously. I should say all but Sharon, who only sometimes joined in to relieve her glaucoma. She was always an enthusiastic social participant, ready with a laugh, joke, or comment.

Not without some regret, I left for Mexico. Soon after arriving, I received a letter from Phil Hefferton inviting me to perform in a concert in Los Angeles with him, Charlie Simon (now Charlie Nothing), and our favorite drummer, Richard Scott. Richard was from Staten Island and played at my New York studio with the above mentioned group on a regular basis. The quartet was to open in a large, well known Los Angeles venue, for a popular soul/blues singer. It seemed like it could be fun. I didn't agree right away but the whole group was insistent and I finally signed on.

There was enough lead time to drive up, play the concert, go to Santa Cruz for a short visit, and then return to Mexico. I made all the necessary arrangements in preparation for the trip and then left with just enough time to arrive a couple of days before the concert date. That meant only one night's stop over.

On the way, in the middle of the Mexican desert, my car started to overheat. I pulled into a gas station on the roadside and opened the hood. Steam was coming from the radiator cap. This was a problem the car had never had before. Not being mechanically inclined, I worried that the pressure of the boiling water might crack the radiator. In my ignorance I thought removing the radiator cap would ease the pressure. Little did I realize the consequences of such an action. I put on my gloves and leaned over to loosen the cap. It exploded out of my hand and a jet gush of boiling water shot up and scalded the right half of my face. If I hadn't been wearing sunglasses I would have lost my right eye. Of course the car cooled right down and I drove to a local village doctor who applied salve and told me to go to the hospital in Monterey. My face was blistered and peeling and a strange color. Looking in the mirror was frightening. I decided to drive all the way to Los Angeles without stopping, and wait until then to seek medical attention. The car smelled like a White Castle. I was in severe pain. I drove for eighteen hours straight and got to Los Angeles the next day.

It was mid-morning when I arrived at my friend's residence. They were shocked and distressed to see me in such bad shape. The right side of my face was dripping off and my guts were burning from too much coffee. We left immediately for a medical facility to get my burns treated. I'm not sure if it was a burn clinic or a hospital, but the doctor took one look and told me it was a medical mistake to put grease on my burns. He began peeling the dead skin off with a drill-like sander. After completing the skinning, he wrapped me up like Boris Karloff in "The Mummy," and sent me on my way. I got back to the pad, unpacked, and fell asleep. I slept until the next morning. The concert was that afternoon.

We were a terrible bomb. I played a penny whistle and my bass. It was complete free-style jazz and the audience wasn't in any way ready for it. I performed with my face almost completely bandaged. We were dressed in outrageous costumes – capes, tights, feathers, and sashes. I wore my patched Levis. Not much denim showed through the patches; they looked like they were made out of a patchwork quilt. To say we were completely unprepared for that concert is an understatement. We ran around on stage and into the audience. We did our best to interfere (albeit, unsuccessfully) with the featured artist, an up and coming young black pop singer. The crowd loved him and his band, and fortunately they didn't boo us off the stage. After the concert we all went back to the pad, ate, and I fell asleep again, catching up for the loss of sleep and stress from the trip and injury. When I awoke, I packed up and drove to Santa Cruz, where I presented my damaged self to Sharon. She took me in with great tenderness. It was kind of traumatic to be transformed from a comely featured young man into a hideous ogre in a few seconds. I must confess I had a problem with vanity, and probably still do, but it was brought to the surface by that unfortunate accident. I had a breakdown for a few hours one afternoon. It was after the bandages came off. I couldn't stop weeping. Sharon was patient and kind, and I finally shamed myself into relaxing and getting control. As it turned out the second doctor did a really good job and the scars gradually faded. My beard may have covered the worst of them. I don't know; I've never shaved since then. I knew then I wasn't going to return to Mexico soon and I settled in with Sharon and Lee. We were having a great time hanging with Pat and Nancy.

After a while Sharon wanted to move up to the mountains above Santa Cruz. She found a very homey little bungalow, two bedrooms, one bath, living room, dining room, kitchen, and a beautiful deck nestled into a redwood tree ring, right above the San Lorenzo River. This tree ring was the leftover result of logging a giant redwood, perhaps fifteen to twenty feet wide, many years before. The house had wooden casement windows all around the dining room. It had French doors opening into the living room off the front porch and French doors in the dining room opening onto the deck. Down by the road was a large two car garage built of solid heart redwood board and bat. There was a spacious redwood deck leading to it from the house. The road ran behind the garage to a one lane bridge over the river. It snaked around off Highway 9 in a series of ninety degree curves that gave us only one neighbor who was very seldom there. These homes were built as vacation cabins in the early part of the twentieth century. The lady across the street still used her small cottage as a rural retreat, but most of the cabins and cottages were now being rented out as income for elderly couples who no longer used them. In the front yard was a very large, incredibly beautiful pink flowering dogwood tree. In the spring it blossomed radiant pink and perfumed the whole yard.

Before moving in I did a bit of redecorating, painting the kitchen walls and cabinets and adding a few minor touches to enhance the bedrooms. It was just a couple of days work, but I noticed that the only traffic going by was the school bus in the morning and afternoon and one or two cars crossing over the bridge on their way home. There was almost no traffic all day as I painted walls and cleaned up in preparation for moving in.

It wasn't long after Sharon, Lee, and I moved in that Pat and Nancy found a house on the corner of our street and Highway 9 only a half block away. Our merry band was together again. I had been given an African thumb harp, a kalimba, in New York and when I showed it to Pat and demonstrated how to play it he started making them. We collaborated, cutting windows in the side of the garage facing the house and a skylight in the roof to let enough light in to use as a studio for us to share. Pat brought his welding equipment over and started work on a musical instrument he was fashioning out of an auxiliary airplane gas tank. He cut a big hole in the tank and strung the hole with guitar strings. The tank was about five feet long, rounded on one end, and tapered to a point on the other. Pat flared out the narrow end in leaf-like caps that he curled and attached several sleigh bells to each leaf. He welded three feet on the round end which became the bottom when it was placed in a standing position. Pat welded a tricycle wheel on the side of the bottom end. Then he installed two lengths of garden hose at the top and electrified it. We hooked it up to an amp and the "Space Bass" was born.

When you kicked the wheel it sounded just like a really good snare drum roll. Two people could blow through the hoses at one time. The guitar strings could be plucked and the tone varied by hugging the body of the instrument. All told, some thirteen people could play the Space Bass at once.

We installed used windows in the front wall of the garage. We cut a hole for a stovepipe. Two windows opened for the summer and latched closed for the winter. We built a desk top to hold my recording equipment and Pat donated a large round red Coca Cola sign, which when struck by homemade mallets was a wonderful gong. We hung the Coke sign from the rafters on two wire cables in front of the sliding door which had once been used as an entrance for cars. We made the mallets out of two short pipes wrapped at the ends with rags and taped over with masking tape.

There was a long work bench on the river side of the garage and shelves made out of orange crates on either side of a small sliding window in that wall. From somewhere came an antique mohair car seat on a raised wooden frame. We put that in the middle of the garage in front of the Coke gong and there it was: a studio, a wonderful studio, where I could paint, practice the bass, have sessions, and record them. We put a work table in front of the car seat. We collected assorted chairs and made wooden benches and started having sessions.

I photographed the Space Bass and we created a poster: "The Space Bass, The First Bass in Inner Space." Pat made a lot of kalimbas out of flat tined metal rakes and quarter-inch plywood with beads that rattled on a wire at the open end. Soon there were enough kalimbas to form a kalimba section. We amplified them and the effect was stunning. Now we had enough instruments to supply quite a few people. I had, by this time, grown tired of the elitism of the jazz scene, which led me to experiment with musical instruments that anyone could play without much practice such as the kalimba, simple bamboo flutes, and drums. Thus started my twelve year "Perfect Music" experiment.

I had grown weary of the pressure and rigidity of the music scene. I felt the need to reconnect the roots of jazz to the variations found in the general population. I wanted to bring the thrill of improvised music to the uninitiated layperson. That meant not much competition. I had a young cousin who was attending the experimental Pacifica High School and I was invited to give a musical demonstration. At the occasion I met his teacher, Fred McPherson, who became an enthusiastic fan of my approach. When I decided to have a session I called Fred, a few other friends, and some of my musician buddies, as well as some of my artist friends, and, of course, Pat who was with this project from the beginning. Pat had built the Space Bass in the small earthen square in front of the studio. When it was done we rolled it into the studio. We plugged it in and with thumb harps, flutes, drums, and the gong we were ready for whatever would come.

I decided to have an open session. Anyone who wanted to, could play. I chose Thursday evening as the time to hold the session. Thursday wasn't the weekend and it was a night not very much else was happening.

With no more notice than word of mouth, Pat, Fred, and I waited anxiously on the first Thursday night. Soon, friends, friends of friends, and strangers began to straggle in. It wasn't long before the studio was packed. I was astonished. Incense was brought in and lit. It mingled with the sweet smell of pot. The tape recorder was loaded and set and the amps turned on. There was a pleasant murmur of conversational patter. I cut through it with an announcement, something like this: "I want everybody to be silent for a moment so we can all hear the music of the universe that goes on around us all the time." Of course, being right on the bank above the San Lorenzo River, we could all hear the river burbling below us. The sound was perfect. I continued after a short pause, "Let he who first hears the first note be the first to play it."

There was a stunned silence and then slowly one by one the thumb harps began to enter, then the flutes and drums, and finally the "Space Bass," and then my bass. The song lasted more than an hour. It had peaks and valleys and a real ending. After the ending I gave a short lesson in kalimba playing. "Put it between your knees and play it like a typewriter" I told everyone. "That was perfect. Let's do it again." Once more the thumb harps started the music. After another long piece we listened to the tape playback. It was hypnotically peaceful. Everyone was lulled into a dreamlike state as they listened to what we had done. I again told them it was perfect. I said, "There are no wrong notes in nature's music. It is perfect music."

We had started a little after 8:00 p.m. It was after midnight when the last notes of the recording we had made trailed off. A few folks left but most were still there in the studio — laid back, eyes closed, transfixed by the music. We had a hard time believing we had made such involved, lyrical, melodic, emotional music. After everyone left, Pat, Fred, and I congratulated ourselves on pulling it off. We were ready for sleep. Fred drove away, Pat walked home, and I went up to the house and crawled into bed beside Sharon and fell immediately into a deep sleep.

The next Thursday I didn't even call anyone and it was more crowded than before. This time a tall, well-built African American conga drummer came. He was huge. His name was Marcellus. He brought his dog, a Great Dane, who sang with the Space Bass. People danced and sang. We had rigged up some blinking colored lights. It was sensational. Afterward we listened to what we had done, with the same effect. It was infinitely calming, mesmerizing, and produced a trancelike mental state which was humorous, peaceful, and refreshing. This became the pattern. We played usually just two songs, sometimes only one long one, and then we would listen to it played back on the tape. I always started us off with a moment of silence listening to the sound of nature's perfect music. "Let whoever hears it be the first to play it."

No matter how crowded or loud the session was, there was never any disturbance, any fighting, or any negative behavior. Not once in twelve years of four Thursdays a month was there ever a problem. Due to the location there was never a complaint from the neighbors. There was never any advertisement, never any public notice, never an empty night. Everybody just showed up every Thursday. All I had to do was open the studio, turn on the lights, the tape recorder, and the amps, and people showed up. In the winter on cold Thursdays I would chop wood in the afternoon and get the potbelly ready to light. Almost always, no always, someone brought weed to smoke. I kept of pitcher of water filled and glasses ready. The water came from the tap or the garden hose and before it got there, from mountain springs. It was a delicious, slightly sweet and clean tasting drink. I used to say, "Have some sweet mountain water." Sometimes folks brought wine or beer but never anything stronger. No one ever got drunk, not once in twelve years of Thursdays.

Quite often professional musicians would come for the liberating quality of the experience. It was so rewarding for them to play with other people, some of whom had never played music before in their lives — rewarding and thrilling for all of them.

The war in Vietnam was still raging, Johnson was President, and huge public peace demonstrations were beginning to happen. I attended the first large scale protest in Berkeley at the University of California Berkeley campus. I brought my sixteen

millimeter movie camera and filmed it. I shot three or four rolls
of film. While there I met another cameraman. His name was
Chick Callenbach. He asked me if I would let him use some of
my film for a documentary he was making about the massive
demonstration. There were many thousands of people attending. There was one speaker after another all afternoon. I didn't
have sound but Chick did and was recording as well as filming.
He asked me if I would like to help him edit the film. I readily
agreed.

We worked in Chick's basement studio in Berkeley. The film
was black and white. It was my first time using more or less
professional equipment. Chick was easy to work with and we
got along well. It took us a couple of months to get the job
done. Chick had a pronounced sense of humor — it showed up
in his documentary — but it was not appreciated by the folks in
the student movement who organized the demonstration. The
movie was panned by them and went down in flames. I thought
they were a bit oversensitive. The humor was soft humor, not
really making fun of the movement, just showing a lighter side of
the action from a few brief shots. For me, it was a great learning
experience but eventually disappointing. In retrospect I feel
the documentary was much too long with not enough real up-
close action. Filming in a crowd like that, it was difficult if not
impossible to get up close. It did give me a lot of good experience
which I was able to put to use in a later adventure in film making.
That was a documentary I made of a young people's collective
that had taken up squatter's rights in an abandoned tourist
motel on the river between Ben Lomond and Felton.

These were young people, many of whom had been kicked out
of their parents' homes for wearing their hair long or for smoking
pot, or who were broke and homeless. One of those residents was
a wild looking man who called himself "Wavy Gravy." Trading
on his image, he later became famous as a spokesman for the
"hippie" movement. Giving credence to his name, Wavy Gravy
had long curly red hair and a wiry red beard that came half
way down his chest. He was a friendly, good natured, clownish
fellow with a collection of wry and witty slogans to match any

occasion. Sort of a down-and-out Will Rogers.

During the 60's, four large social movements came together: the anti-Vietnam war peace movement, the environmental movement, the Black Civil Rights movement, and the Women's movement. The combination of these social movements helped to create an exciting, positive air of freedom and progress in America. It was a populist response to the assassination of President Kennedy, the awful human toll the war was taking on both sides, and the long overdue civil rights of African Americans and women. The American people were rising up. Between Sharon and me, we were active in all these movements.

There was also an organic farming movement embedded in the environmental cause. Alan Chadwick was holding forth at U.C. Santa Cruz with a large organic garden and a crew of disciples. I did some filming of this garden and soon some of his students started a "French Intensive" garden on four acres right around the corner. Jim Nelson and Beth, his wife at that time, were the leaders of this endeavor.

Jim and I became friends and I gladly participated in their struggles to gain community acceptance. Soon they were providing a vegetarian diet for sixteen families on their four acre plot, named "Camp Joy." It was amazing and inspiring. Jim is still, after all these years, holding forth on the farm.

At that same time, the Army was tearing down some old World War II barracks on Angel Island in the San Francisco Bay and Jim somehow got permission to do the work, and in return claim the lumber from this project. He arranged to transport the lumber from the island to the mainland on a ferryboat. I played a small part in that project, going out to the island to film and help with the careful deconstruction/salvage project. We brought the wood back to the Camp Joy farm on ancient lumber trucks. Jim and his crew built a large, handsome house for themselves with it. Those were heady times. We literally were "turning swords into plowshares." If I have ever met one moral giant in this life of compromise, it is Jim Nelson. His life and steadfast purpose and energy have long been an inspiration to me. While caring for my ailing mother in the 1990's I produced a series of paintings from drawings I did at the Camp Joy farm. We had a show of this work at the Boulder Creek library. Many of the paintings and drawings are still on the walls of the Camp Joy farmhouse.

But I digress. Let's go back to the sixties and the founding of a youth commune on the San Lorenzo River. Although they were a scruffy lot, I admired their courage. They were experimenting with the barter system and a free dropped-out social order. They were young, full of idealism, and into trying something new. It was definitely outside the mainstream.

It wasn't a nudist camp but there was a lot of nude bathing in the shallow rapids of the river. The water was cold and clean in the summer and shallow enough for small children to play in. The beach was private and far from the road so the children played in the nude and moms and dads watched them, also in the nude. Now there may have been older people living nearby but I couldn't see any houses from the beach, so if they were offended they would have had to walk through the woods and hide in the bushes to get a peek of this bare action. Apparently some did and an elderly cop was called who hid in the bushes and took Polaroid pictures of the bathers. We knew him as "Shakey Jake." It was said he had a drinking problem which caused him to tremble until he got off duty and had his first drink. He would show up from time to time, come out of the bushes, and order everyone out of the river. The young folks would taunt him mercilessly until he finally pulled his gun and threatened to arrest everyone. Then, begrudgingly, everybody would traipse off wrapping towels around themselves or putting on their scanty summer outfits.

These people were trying to turn on and drop out as Professor Leary had suggested. They had a community based on democracy and run on consensus which they arrived at in weekly meetings. They had an older married couple who they looked up to and sought leadership and counsel from. They were using their lives to resist the war, the system, and a social order they no longer believed in. Soon the local press took notice of them and dubbed their commune "The Holiday Cabins," after the old name of the dilapidated commercial tourist court. Many letters to the editor of the local paper featured the subject of The Holiday Cabins, some positive but most negative.

Some commune members came to my perfect music sessions, which made me aware of them before their notoriety in the press. I visited their camp at their invitation and found it a charming, honest experiment in a peaceful social movement. I thought their plight could be helped by a movie showing the beauty and positive nature of their attempt. I attended their weekly meetings and presented them with my ideas. After a couple of meetings with much open discussion they agreed to allow me to film them in somewhat intimate detail. I advised them not to invite anyone else to join in this filming project so as to avoid possible exploitation. My plan was to make a documentary film which possibly would earn them some income.

A little before this project I had written a short piece which I called "The Paradise Proclamation." I recorded myself reading this piece and mixed in a perfect music tract behind it. "The Paradise Proclamation" declared that the earth was the Garden of Paradise. To my mind, this was obvious simply by observing the balance of the incredible diversity on this planet, all made possible through the complex interactions of nature. I also stated that when human social evolution is denied it creates revolution. I compared the foreign policy of our nation to "a drunk in a bar trying to pick a fight with a Chinaman."

At this time, I was the host of a jazz radio program on which I sometimes played perfect music tapes. I also played "The Paradise Proclamation" on this program. I felt that if people only realized how beautiful and perfect nature was, perhaps they would take better care of it. I said the only thing wrong with the earth was what we had done to it. These ideas led me to name the documentary project "Beachhead in Paradise."

It was the time of huge music festivals. The time of Woodstock, the Monterey Pop Festival, and the Newport Jazz Festival. I tried to take the Paradise concept international. I wanted to have a "Paradise Pageant" which would put the stamp of Paradise all across the planet. I sent a tape to the Beatles, hoping they would see and understand the value of this concept. I never received a reply but shortly after this, their recording of "Revolution" was released.

Meanwhile back at the Holiday Cabins, I thought a small local music festival would be a nice climax to the film we were making.

There were a few musicians living up in the Santa Cruz Mountains. Most were rockers.

There was a pretty good band just around the corner on Highway 9 that I was friends with. They agreed to participate in the mini-festival. I put together a perfect music jazz band and we planned a finale of perfect music to end the festival with as many participants as possible. I brought this plan before the weekly meeting at the Holiday Cabins and, as you might expect, found no opposition to it. Again I stressed not letting anyone else film this festival. I had high hopes for this mini-Paradise Pageant and wanted exclusive rights to the film for the commune and myself.

On the big day of the festival, Pat and I loaded up the Space Bass, my bass, and the filming and recording equipment and drove down to the Cabins. When we got there, we discovered another filmmaker setting up. I already had several hours of film in the can so there was no possibility of turning back. Now this guy had much better equipment than I did. We set up our equipment and the music started with the rock band. I stayed very busy – playing, filming, recording, and keeping things going. What I didn't see or know about until after it was all over was that this other filmmaker was passing out LSD and filming the kids taking it. He also brought a large stash of grass and filmed a phony deal that he set up for a dramatization of the sale of this grass. This was a complete falsehood, set up and filmed by this intruder. The outcome of this fabrication was that he sold that part of his film to a national news agency which in turn played it all across the nation on T.V. news programs.

After this appeared on T.V., the local police became much more interested in "The Holiday Cabins." I showed my film around, first at the Cabins, then at various gatherings around the county. I spent about ten grand on this project and didn't receive a penny back. Eventually the cabins were burned to the ground by the police and fire departments. This was an example of just the kind of exploitation I had warned about. It was also, ironically, the very type of slick social-order propaganda the kids were trying to drop out of.

I can't really say that my efforts had any effect, but shortly after his election Nixon went to China, and America no longer appeared to the rest of the world, "like a drunk in a bar trying to pick a fight with a Chinaman." I don't pretend to have had anything to do with Nixon's decision to go to China but it has always seemed rather coincidental. Nor can I say that the Beatles' hit "Revolution" was their answer to my request for their help in staging a world.wide "Paradise Pageant," but if it was it shows that they didn't listen very carefully. What I said was not that I wanted a revolution but rather that I wanted evolution to be unhampered and occurring naturally at its own free pace.

Anyway, be that as it may, the "Paradise Pageant" folded after the first and only local one, invaded and destroyed by this unknown interloper posing as a hippie and exploiting, for his own personal gain, the hard work and sacrifice of all the kids and us locals. I still can't help wondering what could have happened if millions of people had gotten together world-wide to proclaim the earth as "the Garden of Paradise" and began insisting all nations treat it as though it was.

One other larger scale event that I participated in was the first rock and folk festival in Monterey. Pat and I brought the Space Bass down there and set it up outside the arena/stage area in the open free space surrounding the main stage. We began playing and soon drummers and flute players began drifting in to join us. We started out having people play empty beer and pop cans like bongo drums. Soon there were several hundred participants in perfect music and we began to drown out the loud speakers from the stage. It was sensational.

Lovely ladies in exotic costumes were dancing all around us; people were singing free style and chanting. The energy was monumental and the song lasted for almost three hours. It was a symphony of perfect music. I shall never forget it. After it ended, we were exhausted. Pat and I packed up and went home as the sun was setting.

Another time I was up in San Francisco at a Santana's big band concert, which I think was being held at the Fillmore. I had my penny whistle with me and found my way to a balcony box above one side of the stage. The band was really cooking. I started playing my brass penny whistle like a piccolo, riding high above the band with trills and obbligatos. Santana's sound was coming out of giant speakers on the stage and I thought I was just playing for my own amusement, but it sounded pretty good to me. Soon, I noticed some of the guys in the band looking up at the balcony trying to figure out where the flute was coming from. They were smiling so I kept it up and really got off.

Another time I led a large group of players and a chorus of around twenty men and women singing and playing a tune I had composed. We were on an island in a Santa Cruz city park which was surrounded by a duck pond. The island was appropriately called "Duck Island." The band had some well-known jazz musicians in it as well as many neophyte players from the Thursday night perfect music sessions; and this was yet another very rewarding experience.

I began producing thematic art shows. I had a show of portraits of women I had drawn; they were young women, middle-aged women, and old women, all friends of mine. It was shown at the Santa Cruz Library, which was serving as the Santa Cruz Art Museum.

I drew a sketch of the rapids in the San Lorenzo River at the site of the police action and the nude bathing at the Holiday Cabins. Then someone in the logging trade brought me a ten inch slab cut out of the center of a mid-sized redwood tree that extended down to the root ball and had beautiful burl grain. The grain inspired me to transfer the drawing of the rapids, much enlarged, to the scale of the slab. Before I could do this I had to sand the surface smooth. That took me about six months of just sanding several days a week until I got it smooth enough to carve. I did this work on the back deck of the house across the street which my mother had bought and which I remodeled for her. When I finally had it smooth enough, I put the drawing on it and then carved it out in relief with several Dremel drills which would burn out after a few months of use. When the carving was done, I coated the face, sides and back of the slab with multiple coats of polyurethane.

During this time the county had purchased the land the burnt down Holiday Cabins had been on along with a mansion adjacent to the property from which the complaints had come. The elderly owners had passed on and their heirs put the mansion and land up for sale. When I finished the carving I was offered a display cupola at the head of a nature walk on this land, designed by Fred McPherson, which wound down to the river and back. It stayed there until it was vandalized. Someone had taken it down and hidden it in the bushes nearby. Fred called me and told me the sculpture was missing. I went down and found it, undamaged, in the bushes near the cupola. I got someone to help me carry the slab to my pickup and hauled it back to my mother's house and installed it in her dining room instead. The drawing I worked from was used as the cover of the booklet that went with the nature walk project.

Then there were the full moon festivals that were held on the night of the full moon in good weather. These gatherings took place on a mountaintop meadow on a piece of property my friend Brad Blanchard owned. Folks would start to gather at the meadow at dusk. The road up to it was impassable after a while and a short walk through the woods was necessary to get there. People would straggle in, in small groups, bringing food and drinks. A bonfire was built in the center of the meadow. Both Brad and I brought thumb harps, drums and flutes. Folks brought horns. Marcellus brought conga drums and his big dog. As the sun went down the drums would start. The fire was lit. People would start cooking on it. Firewood was gathered in the afternoon by those of us who came early. There was always a rich soup, sometimes barbecued deer or goat or chicken, water, beer and wine, but no hard liquor or hard drugs.

These were really magical happenings. Sometimes hundreds

of people came, sometimes only a few dozen or less but each one was a celebration of freedom, nature, humanity, and the cosmos. I might add that marijuana, LSD, peyote, and magic mushrooms all at one time or another were used in these celebrations and not once was there ever any trouble or violent behavior of any kind.

I had a favorite pair of Levis that fit just right but were beginning to develop holes. I started sewing patches on them but in time it got to be too much trouble. Sharon couldn't patch them because of her visual problem but I couldn't bring myself to discard them. Pat's wife Nancy volunteered to keep them going for me and under her hand they gradually became a work of art. I wore these pants at all the Thursday night perfect music sessions and all the events the perfect music band played; they were my perfect music performance uniform.

The Space Bass

There has always been one "Perfect Music" session that remains indelibly fixed in my memory. I'd like to take this opportunity to try to describe it for you. Although I have the session recorded on tape, I can't really remember what month or year it took place, but I do remember the evening very clearly.

The night started out quietly as usual with Pat and me setting things up and getting the studio ready. Pat tested out the Space Bass to make sure all its features were in place and working. I plugged in the mikes and tested them on my tape recorder and made sure it would roll. We then distributed kalimbas, flutes, and drums around the studio.

While we were involved in this task the gentle whisper of the river was interrupted by the sounds behind the studio of several vehicles – two cars and an old pickup truck. Doors slammed and footsteps crunched on the gravel crossing the street. The fence door at the back side of the studio opened as the procession of this evening's players thumped single file across the narrow boardwalk in front of the window over the work bench. I recognized every one, all were friends. The group included Futzie

Nutzle, a fine draftsman and cartoonist, Bruce Dreffer, a friend of both of us, a carpenter whose name I can't remember, and several other mutual friends. They knocked; I told them to come in. If no music was playing people knocked, not knowing for sure if it was really happening. Neither Pat nor I knew the answer to that question until people showed up, but they did for an uninterrupted twelve years of Thursdays. That's approximately six hundred and twenty-four Thursdays.

Still it was always a guess whether anyone at all would show. We never advertised in any way other than the few phone calls we made for the first one. We just got the studio ready and waited for the faithful to come, and they always did. In the winter it was necessary to have a short stack of firewood next to the potbelly stove, but this night was a cool, dry evening in the early fall. The air was soft and fragrant with the spicy smell of redwood trees. The river was singing a friendly burble.

Our friends entered and we exchanged greetings; joints were rolled and lit. Soon more people arrived and the studio, now fragrant with pot smoke and incense, began to fill up. Pat hooked the Space Bass up to a speaker which he turned on. I started the tape recorder and we were ready to go. I gave my ritual pre-starting instructions, "Let us all be still and listen to the song that is always playing," then after a short pause in which the river asserted its gentle presence, I continued, "Let whoever hears the first note be the first to play it."

This short invocation always produced a momentary heightening of pressure, a certain self-consciousness, a feeling of "Who, me?" The weight of this tension would grow quickly until someone broke the silence. Then the music would simply flow out of everyone like a water faucet being turned on. One by one all were drawn into the song. This wasn't wishful thinking; I witnessed it every Thursday night for the twelve years I conducted "Perfect Music" sessions. Now I should mention that the carpenter who came this evening had never before played music of any kind. The young man driving the pickup was a very courageous fellow who had stood with me, defying bulldozers clearing and grading through a meadow for a new bypass route. I was there to film the travesty. I wanted to get a shot straight into the huge bulldozer as it moved toward us.

The tension continued to build until Pat came in softly strumming the strings of the Space Bass. I followed with a kalimba and soon all were involved. We were rolling! Everyone in the studio was playing. Several people joined Pat on the Space Bass. Flutes were twittering bird-like, or riding above it all with longer notes and sustained melodies. More participants joined me playing kalimbas, following my simple instructions, "Put it between your knees and play it like a typewriter." Now we had an amplified kalimba section. The studio was throbbing. We were all floating in the air, at least that's what it felt like. Underneath it all the river kept up its sustinato, momentarily drowned out, but like a bass line anchoring everything to the earth. We throbbed, we buzzed, self-consciousness was completely overcome, there were no wrong notes. This was as close to Paradise as it's possible to get. We were truly experiencing "Perfect Music," we were making it happen! Men and women getting together, trusting one another and letting it rip. No rehearsal, no score, no key, no rules, perfect music, perfect freedom. It was like a dream but we weren't dreaming; this was as real as it gets. What I call "real reality."

As I mentioned earlier, there was a large, five foot in diameter, metal Coca Cola sign suspended from the rafters behind the throne-like Model T car seat. It was curved at the edges and produced a wonderful gong sound with majestic overtones that hummed for a long time after it was struck. We had hollow steel tubes wrapped with rags at one end to soften the blows, which we used to play the gong. When striking the gong rapidly with two of these homemade mallets it was possible to produce a drum roll sound-sensation which buried each stroke in the massive vibrations they were creating. By this technique the sound could build into a thundering roar.

Now that the kalimba section was fully established and several people were on the Space Bass, I switched to the string bass and Pat picked up one of his homemade flutes to join me in a duet. After this I picked up my soprano sax and blew a solo cutting through with the sharp edge sound of the horn. Then as the music reached full volume I moved to the gong and started the roll I described, softly at first but slowly building to a fortissimo roar as the music climaxed.

I let the gong's roar gradually subside and noticed a kindred note sustaining from it. Then I recognized what it was. It was the engine of the pickup as, unbeknownst to me, the young fellow that drove it had left the session and was turning around and shifting up the hill in the street behind the studio. The sound caught everyone's attention. It was so perfectly appropriate. That old motor was singing like a bird as it turned around and shifted up the hill. The gong faded slowly, all other sounds stopped and we all just listened as the old engine pulled up the hill and faded out of hearing, disappearing into the night. Only the river continued. I turned off the recorder. We all looked at each other after a prolonged silence and then broke up with laughter. What a thrill! It was indescribable even as hard as I have tried to find words for it. It was miraculous!

We immediately listened to it on the recorder and were just as impressed or even perhaps more so. Everyone left only after the whole tape was over. Later Nutzle and I decided to do a joint illustration of the pictures the music inspired in our imaginations.

We named the song "The Legend of the Indian Dog Man of the Cosmos." The legend goes something like this: In an Indian village next to a cornfield a white dog with black spots realizes that to this tribe dog meat is a delicacy. He comes to the conclusion that he must transform himself and become and Indian. With the help of meditation and a little herb he manages to transform into a spotted, floppy eared Indian brave. The Great Spirit notices him and his astonishing feat and presents him with a solar powered flying automobile. This is a huge thrill for the Indian Dog Man, who immediately takes off and tests out his new wheels. He flies around in the cosmos getting more and more excited, and eventually goes so fast that he and the sun car melt down and disappear.

Nutzle and I just sat down in the studio and, listening to the tape, started drawing on three large pieces of poster board. Not much was said until we had finished the project. When we had filled up the three panels, we analyzed the drawing and came up with the title for the piece and the legend to go along with it. If this seems a bit like a backward process, well that's for sure the way it was done.

Our idea was to use these three panels to create a fold-out poster to go inside a long-play record and use a part of one of the panels as a cover for the album. That was the drawing of the Dog Man with goggles and a World War I leather helmet, ears flying out in the breeze behind him, driving the sun car through the cosmos. Unfortunately this project, like so many others, has never come to fruition, but I still have all its pieces and the hope that some day it will. It was truly a miraculous evening and one incredibly beautiful experience I would love to share with the rest of the world.

Part III

The Hip Pocket Bookstore, Fall 1964

4. Peter Demma

I interviewed Peter at a cafe in downtown Santa Cruz in 2002. The recording was transcribed by Becky Leuning soon after, and the transcript of the interview posted to our website in 2006. It was edited recently for this volume by Judy Lomba. Peter passed away August 28, 2015, age 78.

Ralph: Where were you were born?

Peter: I was born in Oakland, California and I think I went more or less immediately from thereto Redwood City. I lived at the foot of a hill above Redwood City on which there was a big cross at the top, and there used to be Easter rituals held there each year. But for the rest of the year it was vacant. As a little kid I used to wander all around this huge, huge hill with not a house in sight; I got to see that entire hill covered with grass, and to go down it on a giant grass sled that my father built, which I fell off of and it ran over me. I think that's probably when my mother decided that was it, she's no longer going to be married to this alcoholic, motorcyclist, crazy Dane. Close scrapes, man – how did I last this long? You'd be surprised at the places I've been and how I survived. Lord only knows I must have a mission. That's what I thought. I've been thinking that more and more.

Ralph: You thought you had a mission when you were in school?

Peter: Yeah, I always thought I had a mission, even when I was three years old. Hah. What makes a person like that? Like the Blues Brothers or something.

Ralph: Public schools in Redwood City, California?

Peter: My mother separated from my father just after my sister was born; then she went to live with her folks in Berkeley, and that's where I grew up. I was around seven or eight years old. I used to run around the streets of old Berkeley. We called it old, and it was old. It would be old to anyone. It was a lot of fun. We were terrorists.

Ralph: We're talking about 1940s now.

Peter: Mm-hmm. I went to the movies twice a week, Saturday and Sunday at least. I was really programmed by all those movies. I thought I was John Wayne for many years. It was just recently that I finally had to admit to myself that I really wasn't John Wayne at all. That's really fooling yourself all those years.

Ralph: So public schools in Berkeley then, all the way?

Peter: I went to a convent in my first and second years. Nuns.

Ralph: First and second year of–?

Peter: Grammar school. And then in my first and second year of high school I went to a Jesuit college prep in San Jose: Bellarmine. Then I transferred to Menlo Atherton and graduated there in 1955.

Ralph: Your mother was moving around these towns?

Peter: No, she remarried. That's why my name is Sicilian and not Danish.

Ralph: What was the Danish name?

Peter: Huderbol. It was a cockamamie irreproducible, first-time-use name that my grandfather came up with because he wanted to change his name from Hanson – there were far too many Hansons per capita in Denmark like there are, say, Changs in Peking.

Ralph: So you were Peter Huderbol for some years and then you became Peter Demma –

Peter: Can you imagine that little kid out in the fucking play area, "He's a butterball, butterball."
Ralph: So your mother remarried and –

Peter: Made my name Demma, and then no one made jokes about me anymore.

Ralph: And then they moved through these different towns, like Menlo Park.

Peter: Yeah, we all moved to Redwood City. We moved from one house to another, staying with my stepfather's relatives, until we had our own house, which was in suburban Redwood City just outside of downtown.

Ralph: Now tell me how you got from high school there to Istanbul.

Peter: I joined the Air Force.

Ralph: Ah-ha. After graduating from high school.

Peter: Yeah. I put in some time at Lockheed and the Marine Reserve and knocked about different odd jobs, and then finally went to the University of Syracuse in New York to learn Romanian. That's what the Air Force wanted me to do so I could keep track of what was going on in Romania. That was my job after I graduated, and I stayed in Turkey for three and a half years doing that kind of work.

Ralph: Listening to Romanian broadcasting in Turkey or something?

Peter: Yeah, along with other shenanigans.

Ralph: And that's where you began your life-long association with dope.

Peter: Ah. I had no idea what anything besides alcohol was. I drank enough alcohol at a sitting to get a psychedelic experience. I knew what I wanted but alcohol wasn't working. If only there was something else – we would say this to one another. Heavy drinkers we were. Then one night we were outside in a taxi cab with these ladies and they passed this big spliff and it had some hashish in it that was like TNT. At least that's the effect it had on me. And at that time I was an Anslinger baby, you know. I believed that if you smoked a joint you'd get syphilis; it was the last thing you'd want to do.

Ralph: This taxi cab was in Istanbul?

Peter: Yeah.

Ralph: Now this is sometime in the 1950s?

Peter: 1958 -'59. In 1961 I came back to California, saw that my sister had taken up with a fun loving crowd that was living in the Perry Lane area in back of the Stanford Shopping Center. It was through her that I met Neal Cassady, and we struck up a friendship that I'll never forget.

Ralph: He was living there on Perry Lane or hanging out there?

Peter: Well he never really stayed in one place very much at that time, but he'd always light down on Saturday to go out to the horse races.

Ralph: Were Ken Kesey and the Pranksters there or some other group?

Peter: Yeah. They weren't called "Pranksters." They were Ken

Kesey and friends. And I got to meet everyone who was part of that circle and adjacent circles.

Ralph: So meeting Neal Cassady was in 1962 or '63, something like that?

Peter: 1961. Then I shipped out with the Merchant Marine. It's hard to reflect on anything for me, because usually I've felt that the shadow world was a lot more interesting than the straight world.

Ralph: So there are a lot of shadows in your story–

Peter: Well things that probably should stay in shadows... In my case, I've seen things that I said loosely which had to do with my past repeated in court by some adversarial lawyer, where one guy had to win and one guy had to lose, and I wasn't winning at all. And there are areas in the courts where there are no such things as constitutional rights. There is an agency that could be called a gang of thugs, that's the Child Protection Services, and because they can get away with murder they do get away with murder. And they love winning. They have to win. It's either-or. It's not, "Is everybody happy now?"

Ralph: So they can make use of rumors...

Peter: Oh! Bring it up; it doesn't have to have any bearing, it doesn't have to have any relevance, but if someone says, "Well we have it on good authority, Your Honor," then the judge can say, "Okay, I'll accept that." Amazing!

Ralph: Okay. It was Ken Kesey and friends on Perry Lane where you met Neal Cassady around 1961 and now I'm interested in everything from there to Santa Cruz.

Peter: Well, Ron Bevirt, who was to become my partner at the store, was at the time — a couple of years before the store opened — a lieutenant in the army at Fort Ord in special training, and he had a friend who also was in the army, another lieutenant, Norman Gurney.

Anyhow, Ron and I used to do a lot of things together, and I think he was very impressed with my sense of mission. I was destined, ordained, to have a bookstore somewhere. It was written in Napoleon's Book of Fate. I don't know if you're aware of the Napoleon Book of Fate. It was an oracle and I used it to read my destiny, which was that I was to have bookselling as my passion, and I just fell for it hook, line and sinker. I thought, well, not only do I really like the idea of having a bookstore, but it's ordained. It's in the Napoleon Book of Fate. We would go to Big Sur Mineral Springs before it was called Esalen, and get a cabin there and a tent. And we all went together to a seminar down there by Paul Reps, who compiled *Zen Flesh, Zen Bones*.

Ralph: Back to asking you how you got to Santa Cruz — you were, at the time, meeting with Ron Bevirt and going to Big Sur.

Peter: And it had nothing to do with Santa Cruz except coming up to Santa Cruz on mad dashes with Neal Cassady for some reason or another. Driving with Neal is something you would only understand if you actually had the experience, and then it would really mean something to you dramatically.

Ralph: Neal Cassady drove you down and that way you met Ron Bevirt, who was stationed in Fort Ord?

Peter: No. A lot of writers used to hang out on Perry Lane and some of us would get together and go to the mineral springs for the Zen Flesh Zen Bones seminar. In the hot tub one night during that seminar someone suggested, "Why don't you open a bookstore?" By this time Ron Bevirt was gonna have a bookstore at one place or another, Palo Alto, somewhere, because he liked the idea a lot.

Ralph: Because he was getting out of the army.

Peter: Uh-huh. They were just about to get out, both he and Gurney. And so he borrowed some money from his folks.

Ralph: This is about 1963.

Peter: Mm-hmm. And we followed up on that suggestion and decided that we should have a bookstore in Santa Cruz, because there was a university going in there and they probably didn't have much that was very exciting yet and there were no bookstores. I had early on determined that my bookstore was going be like City Lights or something really hip, you know? And that's one of the reasons the word hip just sort of stuck with us when we decided what to name it. The idea was Mort Grosser's, who wrote *The Discovery of Neptune.* He said, "Why don't you call it the Hip Pocket Bookstore?" We were all sitting around–

Ralph: So he was on Perry Lane also?

Peter: Oh yeah. Many people hung out there. Larry McMurtry – all kinds of people. I got to meet a lot of people. Anyhow, we thought that was just a peachy-keen idea and Santa Cruz was gonna be the place. We came up to Santa Cruz and I saw this old diner that had been abandoned and was just gathering dust. It had been run by a Yugoslavian not too long before and used by Republican campaigns or something from time to time but otherwise it was just pretty much vacant. So that's where we decided to have the bookstore. We secured that and started packing the thing with books. We had enough room not only for a bookstore but also an art gallery among other things. And it was one time that Santa Cruz had a really decent art gallery where there was a lot of fun and that people enjoyed going to.

Ralph: So how did Ron Boise enter the picture?

Peter: Well, I said, "Gee, what should we have for a sign?" to Ron Bevirt—this was at the time we were planning to have a bookstore somewhere, anywhere, and he said, "Look, I know this guy, he said he'd make us one." He had met Ron Boise prior to my meeting Bevirt. And so I got to meet him, he came to Santa Cruz, and he said, "Well, do you have a logo for the store?" And I said, "Yeah, our logo says 'Books for the Imagination' and it has this rune and the rune looks like two figures holding hands. This is the rune for mankind." And Ron said, "Well since it looks like it represents two figures holding hands, why don't we just put two figures up and that will be your logo?" That sounded great, so we bought $600 worth of copper and he put this man and women up. It had been shown at the first Cabrillo Music Festival, and people from there were invited to attend a rare display of the original Kama Sutra sculptures that were being shown at Vic Jower's Sticky Wicket. The Sticky Wicket was a little protohip manifestation where the golf link is to the right of Soquel going south, between that and the freeway. There used to be a turn-off onto the freeway where you could get off, but they shut it down and built this golf link. And so that destroyed the Sticky Wicket. It wasn't easy to get to anymore.

Ralph: A restaurant or cafe or something?

Peter: Uh-huh. And it's where all the Bohemians would hang out.

Ralph: Proto-hip. So this is a year or two before you started the bookstore. And what's his name?

Peter: Vic Jowers. And Sydney, his wife.

Ralph: So Ron Boise had already done his Kama Sutra sculptures and they were on display at the Sticky Wicket.

Peter: Not only that but he had been busted in a big constitutional issue case, a first amendment issue, and at the music festival I met his attorneys and Marshall Krauss and his wife. There was so much magic from that time through 1967, magic

magic magic, of all different kinds. It was so thick. What is it? Is it something that happens to your mind where you see things as magical? It was all Lord of the Rings and the Two Towers.

Ralph: So this is now 1964, maybe.

Peter: We opened in 1964 and Patricia Dunn and Tony Maggi were our first employees. And everything was pretty mellow, but then as time went on it was harder and harder to crack the nut of "How are we going to pay the rent?" and "I'm not getting as much..." and that's when I met Leon Tabory. Neal said, "I have a friend. He's got some money and he's looking for someplace to put it. He'd like to get involved in this area. I'll send him over to meet you." So Leon came, thought about what was going on, and said, "Well, maybe I can give you a few ideas. Why don't you do something like what they're doing up in the city right now, a free speech night?" And I said, "Gee, that's a great idea. Okay, let's do it." So we started our little circle and it grew really big. At first we'd meet in the gallery, but it grew so big that we had to move out of the store and find a larger building somewhere to meet.

Ralph: It was a program of once-a-week presentations of an author?

Peter: Every Friday night I'd put bright fluorescent poster paint letters in the window of the store announcing what the subject was going to be. One day the subject was marijuana, and there it was in big letters – you know how these fluorescent paints, when set off against one another, they just kind of vibrate — well the whole window was done like that. "Tonight's subject will be MARIJUANA!" And that's before anyone besides ethnics and musicians and gangsters had anything to do with marijuana. That was when Leon conducted his seminar, the first marijuana seminar probably he'd ever given on the West Coast. He instructed everyone about what it was, and asked them to consider the possibility that people in their own families were going to be involved with it, that it was getting so popular in leaps and bounds that there was no stopping it.

At that time there were a lot of ultra-conservative groups that met regularly in Santa Cruz, like the Weathermen and the John Birch Society, and they all were upset that we had the audacity to start what we did and how did we get here and what was going on anyway and it looks like this is the beginning of the end, the beginning of the apocalypse. I'm talking about the honchos, you know, big number-one generals, jeffes. Like Dr. Stan Monteith, a hard-core republican. These guys, some of them had automatic weapons and they worked in the sheriff's department, and they had regular meetings and bivouacs. They did a lot of funny things; they were wackos. But we were the weirdos. And when Leon laid it on them that marijuana was going to be the next big deal in this little town, everyone was in a state of shock. They just could not take that. They started quoting the Bible and they'd stand up and claim that only the Lord was ordained to make true chemicals. We said, "What do you mean by true chemicals?" We had our own concerns. All this was leading up to an incident where we were arrested for a photography show that we gave. The local liberals didn't come to our aid and champion our cause or anything. They just sort of turned around and said, "We don't know these guys." But I won the hearing in that case. They had no right to shut our show down; there was nothing that was obscene. One of the items that was confiscated was a photograph of a cabbage cut in half and you could see all the erotic things taking place in the design of that cut cabbage. That was evidence.

Ralph: I think we have skipped over the story of the opening and the mayor pulling the sheet off the sculpture, so could you fill me in on that?

Peter: Norman Lezin, the mayor, said sure, he'd be glad to unveil the sculpture — because at that time we were looked upon as champions of some kind or another, you know, for opening up this new bookstore. That was before they found out they'd never get to know us or even want to. Ach! Santa Cruz was already really cliquish, but at that moment everyone was in a state of surprise and thrall. We had the Beatles singing "I Want to Hold Your Hand" through a sound system that projected outside — and that's another thing about the store: you couldn't be anywhere near it and not know it was there because there'd be this music blasting out that you wouldn't hear anywhere else. Where else would you hear the Supremes on Pacific Avenue? So "I Want to Hold Your Hand" was blaring out over the speakers; there were literally throngs of people there. Then the police came up in a flying wedge on motorcycles because they had a warrant for someone who had been seen at the celebration there. And they found him, Pat Cassidy, from Big Sur, who was legendary up and down the coast.

Ralph: So the Kama Sutra sculptures had already been on display at the Sticky Wicket–

Peter: I think before that they were at the local gallery managed by Peter Stafford's brother, Michael, and he was arrested also. But I didn't know Michael in those days. He had just come back from a tour in Istanbul; later we'd get together and I'd try to remember my Turkish.

Ralph: So the Kama Sutra sculptures were at the Vorpal Gallery in San Francisco and then they were at Sticky Wicket — then they were moved to the Hip Pocket bookstore?

Peter: No. We never had the Kama Sutra sculptures.

Ralph: The commotion was about the man and woman that Boise made.

Peter: Yeah, I think it was really about the penis. You know, look at where we've come to today. You know the Penis Puppetry show in San Francisco? These are three Australians who make different things out of their penises; there's a big blowup on the screen, it's a two and-a-half hour show. Well, we've come a long way to just see a penis anywhere, that's something you go to Frenchy's for in Santa Cruz, those guys must have been to Golden Gate Park, but I guess they have leaves up there, huh? Don't they? I guess I'm thinking of Europe or something.

Ralph: Do you mean Ron's sculpture of the two figures holding hands, a man and a woman I presume, that the man actually had a penis?

Peter: Yep, had a penis, that's probably what the problem was.

Ralph: It wasn't the topless, it was the bottomless.

Peter: It's just sculpture, but – mapping the territory — those literalists really had a problem. And so this was a little too stark, I guess, for Santa Cruz. But we drop-kicked it into the far west. Used to be you went east for this sort of thing but now Santa Cruz was like going east, but it was far west instead. You couldn't get any further west.

Ralph: So there was an opening for the store and the sculpture with the two figures had a sheet over it and you were there and the mayor came to give a talk...

Peter: And unveiled the sculpture, and Bargetto Winery was hosting the wine. I mean a good time was had by all, and there were throngs — I mean there were a lot of people. And then the police riding out in a flying wedge excited everybody too.

Ralph: And the police arrived in a flying wedge because they had a warrant for arrest for somebody named Pat Cassidy.

Peter: Someone they were told was there, uh-huh.

Ralph: Who was not related to Neal Cassady.

Peter: No.

Ralph: There wasn't a legal case, like you weren't busted for that?

Peter: No, nobody was busted. I don't even think they found Pat Cassidy. I mean we were just so busy having a good time. It was one big party.

Ralph: So did people like the bookstore? Was it open regular hours and people came in and bought books and then you decided which books to buy and put on display and you were a proper bookstore owner?

Peter: Pretty much. And besides that, any book that you wanted, I would personally go up to San Francisco and get for you, once a week. I did this once a week.

Ralph: So at some point you moved to Santa Cruz — you moved your household, you rented something in order to begin putting together the Hip Pocket Bookstore.

Peter: You know, just before I came to Santa Cruz I was asked to manage a store in Mission Hill, San Diego; it was an ancillary of The Nexus, a bookstore/gallery. The manager, Larry McGilvry and his wife, Geraldine, had run into problems for selling *Tropic of Capricorn* by that pornographer who got into all that trouble in Big Sur....

Ralph: Henry Miller.

Peter: Henry Miller, yeah. McGilvry had been arrested and had won that case on Constitutional issues. And so for a short time I managed his art supply store and bookstore annex. And then when I learned that Ron was ready to move to Santa Cruz, I packed up. I was living in La Jolla at the time.

Ralph: Ron Bevirt? Was he active in running the bookstore also?

Peter: To a certain degree, but he was really involved mostly with the activity of setting it up, so there was some time where it was just all my baby.

Ralph: So when I met you, which I believe was March of 1968 –

Peter: One year had gone by and I had become a television repair technician.

Ralph: The bookstore was over when I met you and you were a television repair person and you were married or you had a partner and you'd been together since the beginning of Hip Pocket Bookstore.

Peter: Yeah, since 1962.

Ralph: So she was with you in Palo Alto and La Jolla and came with you. And did she have an active role in the Hip Pocket Bookstore?

Peter: No, it wasn't her shtick at all. I certainly tried, I'd say, "Hey Karen, can you just take care of the store, give me a break?" Naw, she wasn't into it.

Ralph: I can't remember when your children were born.

Peter: Larry was born in 1963. And Melissa was born after I'd had the store for a year.

Ralph: Yeah, so basically you were a family while this whole drama was unrolling.

Peter: Pretty much, yeah.

5. Bob Hall

Bob Hall was interviewed by Ralph Abraham and Peter Demma in Border's Cafe, Santa Cruz, on Tuesday, March 18, 2002. Bob and his brother Charles had a family real estate business in Santa Cruz. Bob died July 27, 2009, age 86.

The Hip Pocket Bookstore

Ralph: Let's talk about where you were when the Hip Pocket Bookstore opened up.

Bob: Yeah, it was about the time Santa Cruz was enjoying, or suffering, the fallout from the Haight Ashbury in San Francisco, when a lot of the communes and collectives were forming here in Santa Cruz; people getting away from the hard drugs that had entered the picture up there. Sometime in that general period Santa Cruz became a hotbed for hippies. Not the Beat generation, but real hardcore flower children and love people.

Ralph: Who were the first hippies that you actually met, people that you knew?

Bob: You!

Ralph: No, before that.

Bob: You know, I don't know. I didn't think of them as hippies then. I just thought of them as flower children.

The Barn

Peter: What can you tell us about the barn?

Bob: Oh, the old barn out in Scotts Valley? That was a fabulous place! I went out there only a few times, but the doctor who did the gold tooth for Ken Kesey — Doctor Smith — he was doing the slides for psychedelic light shows, and the guy that was operating the machine went to get a drink or something and left me in charge of doing the light show and I was going, "Wow! I can do it!" I didn't know Dr. Smith that well but he was quite a character I guess. Did you know him? You must have.

Peter: Yeah, I actually had a tooth extracted by him.

Bob: Did you know him?

Ralph: I did, yes.

Bob: I never got really acquainted with him, but I had fun that night. Everybody was high and everybody was having a wonderful time.

The Beginning

Peter: Well how would you say this stuff in the 60s started here in Santa Cruz? How did it all begin?

Bob: Like I said, I kind of think of it in connection with the fallout of the Haight Ashbury. And I was going up there weekends and spending lots of time at the Kool-aid things that were going on in Golden Gate Park and just walking up and down the street, you know, a boy from small-town Santa Cruz, watching the crowds mill up and down Haight from the park to Ashbury Street, and, you know, wondering to myself, "What's going on here?" Going up into the coffee houses with a little place up above where people were smoking dope and finding a crash pad overnight so I could stay for a couple of days up in San Francisco, leaving my family here in Santa Cruz to wonder where I was I suppose.

Ralph: So the hip scene in Haight Ashbury was well established before anything got started in Santa Cruz.

Bob: To my recollection, yeah.

Ralph: And at that time you had a family with two little children?

Bob: Four. I decided to quit the real estate business and drop out in front of God and everybody here in Santa Cruz and it was a great wonderment to my friends that I had a ponytail and bell-bottom jeans and did the whole nine yards as it were.

Ralph: So was this movement a factor in your dropping out from the real estate business?

Bob: No. That came later when my kids started picking up bad habits at junior high school, finding packets of this mysterious substance called marijuana in their travels around the campus.

Peter: Did they just find them here and there?

Bob: Well that was the excuse I heard from my daughter Robin. I went into her room that she shared with Holly one day and I saw this baggie on the bed and I said, "That smells like..." and I said to my daughter Robin, my middle daughter, "Why don't you roll one up and we'll see if it's any good." Their mother would have had a fit had she known. But I had smoked it and already done some psychedelics up with John Lingemann up on Smith Grade, so I was, you know, I knew the kids would get into it sooner or later anyhow. Those "hippie Hall kids" the teachers used to call them.

Peter: I would think that anybody with any curiosity would be interested.

Ralph: So how did this lead to your quitting the real estate business?

Bob: I got tired after I was married twelve years. I was in the real estate business about ten years and there was just too much family politics, my mom and my wife and my dad. My mom wasn't in the business but she had opinions and I was like the knot in a rope in a tug of war between my mom and my wife, you know; I was being pulled apart.

Psychedelics

Ralph: So it had nothing to do with your discovering marijuana, psychedelics and so on. It was just an internal matter of the family?

Peter: But it freed you up to observe this whole scene, right?

Bob: Yeah, it keyed me up and I got so bold I used to do LSD by going up the river to the Garden of Eden, you know, up the river, because I thought it required more of a contemplative frame of mind, but I got so bold that I would drop a tab of LSD and come downtown and sit at the old Cooper House and listen to the music. And a few people would come up to me and sit down maybe and look at me and get a contact high and say, well, you know, it's no big deal. Here we are on Pacific Avenue listening to Don McCaslin and his Warmth Band and I got rather blasé about the whole thing.

Ralph: Talk about the scene at John Lingemann's place, what was going on there.

Bob: Oh, John of the Mountain. He was a real interesting character. I forget how I met him. Maybe through a real estate friend of mine; he had an office on Mission Street where I had lived for a while after I left my family. They were friends, and I guess he came to visit her one day and she introduced me to him. Can't remember her name. And next thing I knew I was traveling up – where did he live up there? Smith Grade. And found myself in this little cave covered with a tarp that he and his girlfriend had established their place out of. Very strange. You know, they just – he had bulldozers because he was a well digger, and carved this place out of the sandstone and invited other people – other people, you know, Zoo and Tosh and Charlie Nothing and Dude and others to join him while his family lived at the bottom of the hill, his wife and two boys, who were partners in his business. So it was quite a scene.

I was sitting in the cave with him — I call it a cave — and we were talking about this and that and the other thing and he turned to his girlfriend. She was a teacher in Santa Cruz and she dropped out along with him. And Lingemann said, "I think Bob is ready." And of course my antennae went up, tweak tweak tweak. And I said, "Yeah, this is a good place, you know, a beautiful place with a view." And so he gave me a tab and I stood by my car for a while, because I thought, "This is not working. I've got to get back to town, get myself straightened out." And then I got behind the eyeball thing and said, "Oh, I guess I better hang around awhile. I can't drive down the hill." And in the meantime, he and his girlfriend said, "Well, you know, we've got to go shopping today, and why don't you just wander around. There are people here and there you can talk to if you want to, or just hang out here." So I did. It was a very interesting day. And since that time I tell people, to my own amazement, that I never had a bad trip.

Ralph: Yeah, me too.

Bob: Really? I mean I've had incidences that I've been able to manage of paranoia within the process, but I could always bring myself down, even when driving a car, bring myself down to, "Hey, Bob, slow down. Your four tires are not supposed to be off the ground. Ground yourself and get home!"

The Hip Pocket Bookstore

Peter: Did it give you a sense of excitement or anything like that here in Santa Cruz when the Hip Pocket Bookstore opened?

Bob: Oh well, we were all excited about that. I belonged to the ACLU and the first board of directors, we met at Dr. Holbert's home. And I remember one time we passed around nude photographs that had been in the Hip Pocket Bookstore and caused some alarm among the local evangelical gang – we all found them interesting and nothing exceptional. I mean they were very artistic pictures, nothing pornographic about them at all. So then Ron Boise came through town, I guess he lived here for a while, and was doing these –

Peter: My brother was the guy who sold his work in San Francisco and got busted.

Bob: Oh, I remember your brother. So anyway, the upshot of the statue was that everybody, you know, after the story in the paper about this horrible pornographic adventure in–what was it, steel? It must have been about 15 feet tall, a big piece. Right above the entrance to the bookstore. A naked couple. And, you know, first thing anybody would do would be to walk around and find out that what it was that offended the Scotts Valley evangelical people was nothing, you know? You couldn't see anything. Here were these two large sculptures of a man and a woman sort of clinging to each other. I don't remember anything suggestive there. Yeah, a very innocent thing. That's the story about that. And I used to just wander through the Hip Pocket Bookstore.

Peter: What happened as a result? This was brought up in court?

Bob: No, no, no. Never. They just presented them to our board of directors of the ACLU and we passed them around and that was the end of that. We went on to something else. It wasn't the subject of the meeting at all. But that statue, you know, later on, going to Oakland on the mud flats of the Oakland Estuary, I saw one of his other statues that had been put up there, but I didn't realize how many of them he had made. Do you know?

Peter: No. The ones my brother was busted for were actually real small. They were Kama Sutra things.

Bob: Oh, well I never saw any of those.

Ralph: There are still some of them at the Vorpal Gallery... I saw them there just recently.

Bob: I don't remember ever meeting Ron Boise. I know he was around town, but I never had a chance to talk to him. I would have loved to.

Ralph: What about the Odyssey Records and what was going on in there?

Bob: Odyssey Records?

Ralph: The record store, it was next to the Hip Pocket Bookstore, created by Rich Bullock. And Lew Fein had a booth in there where he delivered astrological readings between the books.

Bob: Oh, Lew Fein. He did a reading for me once in his special deck and I bought one of his decks. He was a marvelous guy, a fine astrologer, maybe one of the best I ever met.

Ralph: Still is, I think. I've seen him recently. He hangs out in Boulder Creek.

Bob: You know, I don't know what happened to the deck I bought. It's lost somewhere in storage. He designed it himself, didn't he? I believe he did.

Peter: About the Hip Pocket Bookstore, what other sorts of things were —

Bob: I was fascinated browsing the shelves. Sometimes we would just take books from there into the Catalyst and read them. They must have lost a lot of books during that period. Peter Demma and Ron Bevirt were in the Tom Wolfe story of the Kool-Aid Acid Test, not with their own names, but I knew all the people in that book by their real names here in Santa Cruz — many of them, not all of them.

The Pranksters, yeah. I saw them come through Pacific Avenue, right down the main street of Pacific Avenue going south, when they were fleeing the law and trying to get to the Mexican border, and by God with that psychedelic painted bus, "Further," they were in and out of Santa Cruz like that. I just happened to be downtown at the time and saw this crazy bus. I don't even think I had read the book by that time but I was aware of the Merry Pranksters. And then they were gone. And they made it all the way to the border in that bus with the loudspeaker on the front playing loud music. I mean I don't know how they made it to the border—-

Music

Peter: What about music in the 60s. What was going on here?

Bob: Well, of course my kids grew up with the Beatles and I wasn't terribly fascinated with them. I am devoted now. My kids were not old enough at that point to go to concerts or anything.
Ralph: So what about Max Hartstein? Did you ever go to his garage for perfect music?

Bob: Oh yes. Dear Max. Yes. I loved Max. I used to visit his place up in Ben Lomond and hang out there sometimes. He had a musical group too, didn't he?

Ralph: Yes. The 25th Century Ensemble. It still is far out in the future.

Bob: Well he was living in the present and the future some-how, managing the two very well. Wasn't he a music teacher or something at one time?

Ralph: The first I knew of him he was a professional jazz bass player in a club in San Francisco. And he moved down here from there.

Bob: Charlie Nothing also, up at John Lingemann's place. And they played a few times on their musical instruments made of branches of trees and manzanita and strange instruments that they created, and I heard them a couple times in a little cellar bar down in Capitola, playing there. But Charlie Nothing was also a fine jazz musician out of New York who came to Santa Cruz to drop out I guess. And they played wonderful music and when I was up at the ranch, you know, getting high on acid, I would hear this flute up on top of the hill.

And I would go up there and this was a real cave, you know, going laterally into the hill and I went to the end where there was a little light and a fire and this guy was frying something in a skillet. And I said, "What's cooking?" And he said, "Smoke." He was drying out some marijuana leaves.

And that was Charlie Nothing, and I don't know his real name, but he was a fabulous character. And then, you know, they'd make hand-made flutes and if things got boring in their cave they'd come out and there'd be this one voice, a flute voice, up on top of the hill playing down to another flute or instrument playing in one of the other spots where they were located. You know, they all had their own places but they were separate, one on top of the mountain and somebody down here close to the road. One, Morley was his name, a very fine artist, and I sat in his bus. He had a converted bus for his house. And we were sitting in there. He was in the driver's seat and I was sitting there, and he brought out one of his pictures. I wish I'd bought it.

The Catalyst

Bob: My two daughters, Robin and Holly, worked behind the counter and Eddie was kind of the manager. And I don't think Al and Patti had a bar. But they were still very open to people coming down and playing open mic style every Thursday, I think it was, that they set aside for anybody who wanted to sign up, literally.

Part IV

UC Santa Cruz, Fall 1965

6. Fred McPherson

UCSC talk by Fred McPherson, recorded and transcribed. November 7, 2015.

Introduction by Ronnie Lipschutz, Provost, College 8, UCSC

Today we are going to have a series of discussions and presentations about Utopian Dreaming, and of course here we are at UCSC, the site of so many Utopian hopes more than 50 years ago. Jim Clifford, who is out in the audience, and some colleagues organized a wonderful exhibition about the origins of UCSC — and of course there are these photographs of white guys in suites, being driven around the Cowell Ranch, and presumably being completely mesmerized by it (the alternative was over at the Almaden Valley). I seem to recall the story that it was a hot muggy day over there, and of course over here it wasn't, so they were really captivated by the land. The City of Santa Cruz was really interested in getting the University to come here, and the University was equally interested in locating here — yet I suspect that the city also regretted the decision for a while with all the students and all the related things that have since taken place.

So this is the 50th Anniversary of the founding of UCSC. As part of this 50th-year event, there are various things that have been going on all year. In addition to Ecotopia, one of the inspirations for the conference was this 50-year anniversary, which led to reminiscence about the early Utopian Years of the campus. I wanted to find someone who could speak to that. Of course there are all of the usual suspects, but Barbara Laurence, who has been around for a long time, proposed someone who has been involved since the fairly early years of the campus. He was a student of Page Smith, who, as some of you know, was one of UCSC's founding faculty members and then left. I don't know the full story about that, but maybe our speaker will tell you about it. So, our speaker is Fred McPherson.

I first want to note for those of you who don't know, there are several other Fred McPhersons running around Santa Cruz County, and our Fred McPherson is not those Fred McPhersons. So that is the first thing. The second thing is, since you have the program, and his biography is in there, I am going to be very brief and let him take the floor. The important thing to note is that Fred, and again he will probably speak about it, left the University along with Page. He was working on his PhD at the time, so instead he earned a PhD from Santa Cruz Paideia with Page. He worked on the San Lorenzo River, particularly the restoration of the San Lorenzo River. He continues to teach, and somehow I felt that he would give a much more interesting presentation than one of our, say, more standard speakers. So, I am going to turn the floor over to him. We have titled this talk "Utopia at UCSC, the Early Years," but it is up to him to decide what he is going to say. Thank you very much.

Fred: Utopia at UCSC, the Early Years

We are talking about 50 years ago for UCSC, which you know was founded in 1965. Fifty years gives you kind of permission to go back in time and open the doors and say what really happened in the 60's.

A lot of things about the 60's have been forgotten, deliberately hidden, or misrepresented — a lot of things about the Viet Nam era and psychedelics and those sorts of things people have not wanted to talk about. But that was the era in which UCSC was founded, 1965. So I am delighted and thankful that I do have this chance to be here today and also personally go back in time and think about what that time meant for me and what I was doing there, and how my life fits in with this 50th year anniversary of the founding of UCSC.

Let me just say that in 1965, I was not at UCSC, or even in this area. I was out in the Mojave Desert teaching Biology and doing porpoise research at the Navy Ordinance Test Center in China Lake. I only moved to this area around 1966. I had the opportunity to get away from an environment where they were working on and testing all of the Napalm and other weapons for the war, and to come to this area to be involved in Pacific High School, a school that grew out of the Peace Movement over in Palo Alto. I could tell a lot of stories about the school. It was actually a school that the students and the staff built together. It is still there. Now it is Jikoji Zen Center on Skyline Boulevard (Highway 35) about 2 miles north of where Highway 9 intersects with Skyline. Anyway, it was an alternative experimental high school that we built where the curriculum was, you might say, individualized. Each student had a chance to explore topics that they were interested in by themselves and in groups.

We had a lot of guest groups there. One week we turned the whole school into a Zen center for a week. Another time we invited the Black Panthers up for a visit. One of the guest groups that came to the school for a participatory performance to introduce the students to playing spontaneous "perfect" music was from Boulder Creek. They called themselves the 25th Century Ensemble. They did a perfect spontaneous music session with the students and staff. A group of great musicians brought the Space Bass and other musical instruments. I said to myself, "This sounds like a great group to start playing more music with." They met down in Boulder Creek and I got involved with them playing music on a regular basis. We did lot of benefits around the Santa Cruz area. We would do benefits for the peace movements. Then, here at UCSC, Alan Chadwick came to the campus in about 1966. If you do not know who Alan Chadwick was, he was a very charismatic organic gardener, dedicated to the Rudolf Steiner school of Horticultural and the French Intensive double-digging gardening system. He started the now-famous garden, which is located just below what is now the Merrill College parking lot. The 25th Century Ensemble was asked to come up and do some benefits on the UCSC campus for peace events, anti-draft protests and for the new organic garden. These were still the days of the draft and there were protests against the war and the draft. These events were my first contacts with the UCSC campus and took place about 1968. I thought that it was all just wonderful! I have brought a couple of artifacts with me from that time. (Fred goes to the table and brings back Holly's book and a thumb harp to the podium). These are genuine artifacts from the early days of UCSC.

One is in relation to the photographs and stories in this book that has recently been published by author Holly Harmon. It is titled *Inside A Hippie Commune*, and it deals with the life of the author who, as a teenage girl growing up in the San Lorenzo Valley, lived in a hippie commune at the Holiday Cabins in Ben Lomond. Also, this book is a history and chronology of life in the Santa Cruz Mountains. it is very well illustrated, and has great stories. Here is Suzuki Roshi up at Pacific High School, and stuff about many of the things that went on in that era. It also deals with what happened at the commune, and one of the things that they did was to help with light shows. They would come around to various places like the Barn in Scotts Valley, and that is dealt with here in Holly's book. They'd come to UCSC and a number of other places, and they would do light shows with our local dentist, Captain Outrageous, Dick Smith. The light shows that went on up here at UCSC were incredible.

I just wanted to describe those because they were my first real contact with UCSC. The stories that you may hear about what went on here are maybe different than what I would like to say about them. You know, UCSC when it first started was founded on the idea that it would be interdisciplinary and each of the new colleges that were started would be small, kind of liberal arts colleges which would have faculty from different disciplines on the staff. Some of the people who are here in the audience today were part of those early days. What they would do every so often, maybe once a month, was have a festival celebration of some sort. These would be multidimensional, multimedia, interdisciplinary events that featured music, dance, the arts, the technology of putting on a light show, which is quite involved, movies, slides, and a number of other things that go along with a light show. And these would be held in the dining halls, like at Cowell College or Stevenson when they were first built; and they'd have a big screen on one side and on that screen they would project some of the light show.

Imagine that this is a dining hall here, and you'd have projectors up there, and they'd project a lot of things happening at once up on a large screen and also on the walls all around the room. You could put slides in there about the theme. When we did a benefit for the garden we used lots of pictures of flowers and butterflies and people in the garden.

Sometimes we'd do other ones that would project movies. A big movie that we made and used in light shows was called *Beachhead in Paradise*. And that's now available along with Holly's book. The original movie is on this DVD that was made by Max Hartstein; it featured a big event at the Holiday commune where they presented this first Space Bass in inner space. If you want to see a little bit about what actually happened at that event and what was projected into the the light show, this is a great DVD to look at. So that's one other artifact I bring from that period.

We would usually have a band or bands. Sometimes they were student bands and other times local bands, also described in the book. The same bands that played at the Barn also played here at UCSC. Toward the end of the evening we would start with a moment of silence. Then the thumb harps would start playing, sometimes we'd have two, three or more thumb harps playing. It would be like a choir of thumb harps. And then maybe some of the drums would come in. And then the idea was that whoever heard a note that they wanted to play would just play it. This is called perfect music, and pretty soon dancers would begin dancing, and the light show would be going on, and sometimes we'd just all be going for hours. This thumb harp is made from recycled plywood we found somewhere locally, and these little metal prongs (tines) came from the street sweeper up there in Boulder Creek. Sometimes it would lose them while sweeping, so we had those recycled. You can play it standing up or you can play it by sitting down and putting it between your legs. They have great versatility.

So, out of these wonderful events, some of the richest parts of the early days at UCSC came to me and the community, because when you get everybody together playing music, dancing, celebrating life, celebrating the things that people cared about, and studying to prepare these festivals and then doing them, it would bring people close together, and to me, it really characterized the early days at UCSC.

The 25th Century Ensemble also began getting involved in playing at moon festivals all over the place. In the hills above Aptos, Soquel, Boulder Creek, and Bonny Doon, we'd usually have a moon festival once a month. So between playing all these festivals at the Barn and doing light shows and moon festivals, we had a very active community. Now this also relates to what Ernest Callenbach incorporated into his Ecotopian stories and his vision of Ecotopia. It eventually affected the whole community, and these kinds of events went on all up and down the Santa Cruz Mountains.

Over in Palo Alto, Ken Kesey and his Pranksters were doing them also, and they went on up in San Francisco, and so this became a lifestyle of the Peninsula and the Santa Cruz Mountains.

My main contact was at UCSC with these benefits in the early days, but in 1969 I left Pacific High School life and bought a little house in Boulder Creek. I started to live more over on this side of the hill and got more involved in playing music and things like that, while I was still teaching at Pacific. Eventually I found a job with UCSC Extension. It involved teaching some of the first classes about Human Ecology back in the fall of '69 and the spring of 1970. And then, as there was a growing interest in this area and things were going well at UCSC Extension, I was asked to also be a program coordinator. I started coordinating organic gardening classes throughout the UCSC Extension service area over in Palo Alto and Menlo Park and places like that, as well as over here.

And then, in the spring of 1970, you may remember this, all the Utopian fun, excitement, and opportunities that came with the new campus and the alternative education experiment of the early days of UCSC — all came at a time when the Vietnam War was intensifying. When it was confirmed that the bombing in Laos and Cambodia, that was not supposed to be taking place, was indeed actually taking place, and the extent of the destruction and horror of mass killings of the civilian populations was disclosed to the public, mass protests broke out around the world and particularly on college campuses. There were huge protests on many college campuses, as some of you here may remember, and then from the protests there was a backlash, a reaction from the institutional authorities. There were the killings of students at Kent State University, and when students shut down some of the facilities at Berkeley, and here on the UCSC campus and at UC Santa Barbara, there was this big reaction from the University of California, as you might imagine. There was a lot of fear that things were going to get out of control and that the experiment that had been started up at UCSC was already out of control, and so there was a backlash.

The first Earth Day, 1970

In that spring of 1970, the first Earth Day was scheduled all across America and maybe the world. We planned a big celebration for the event, because we had this great network of people who liked to get together to play music and have festivals and benefits and so forth. We planned a series of events. One event was over at Cabrillo College; Mike Walker coordinated that; one event was down on the Pacific Mall (the beginnings of the Spring Faire); and the other event was supposed to be up here at UCSC. When we got to the celebration at UCSC, there was a band, and we came in with our light show and musical equipment, ready to play, but we were met by a group of police. They were really concerned about what was going to happen. People came inside, saw the police and then turned away. A few people stayed. Any money that was donated we had to give to the police to cover their salaries for the night. No band member, nobody, made any money for that event at all.

When I went back to work the next Monday, my Dean, Dean Tcherendsen, brought me in and said, "There are some things you can do at UCSC and there are some things you just can't do. So we no longer need your services." And oh, I was so heart-broken, because I was just beginning to do the Ecology classes that I wanted to teach and had the opportunity to coordinate the classes for organic gardening that I cared so much about. That same kind of thing happened to other people after that first Earth Day event. So what happened up here at UCSC was kind of the epitome of a backlash to the protests of the late '60s.

I want to say what the characteristics of the early days of UCSC were. I wrote a little list of the founding vision and goals for UCSC. It was supposed to have been like a new, innovative experiment, an alternative experiment in education, where we would have small colleges, kind of patterned after the liberal arts colleges, and they would be independent, but within the context of the whole UC system. So UCSC was deliberately at the very beginning set up to be an alternative experiment. And so from that perspective, they wanted to permit and encourage the staff and students to find new rules and have an opportunity to explore these goals in different, new ways. They were hoping that this would be an example of a new form of education. The idea was that this would then be "the city on a hill" to show the way to other, more innovative, interdisciplinary, multimedia kinds of exploration of learning and student involvement. The first colleges were small. I think the first year, in '65, they only had about 600 students, and even five years later they only had 3,000; now there are about 15,000 students, so things have changed quite a bit in terms of the size of the campus and the number of students, faculty and staff.

So those are some of the size characteristics of the earlier days at UCSC. There were, of course, younger faculty and first- and second-year students. The other theme that was prevalent up here was that you wanted to teach by example. You didn't want to just talk the talk, you wanted to walk the walk. That was the commonly understood way of proceeding. Also, there was great concern about being good stewards of the environment, having sustainability here on campus, and developing the campus facilities in a respectful way in relation to various aspects of the environment.

One of the other innovative things that sort of just happened was that Alan Chadwick showed up. He was not hired by the University. There is a whole story about him coming to the campus that is quite intriguing. Paul Lee eloquently writes about that in his memoir, *There is a Garden in the Mind,* a tribute to Alan Chadwick. So, I suppose if you want to learn more about those days, you could read the book Paul Lee wrote about what happened on the UCSC campus.

After Earth Day

What happened after Earth Day? Well, a lot of things happened to faculty members. Some were denied tenure, and it's not really clear exactly why. Was it because of the anti-war protests? Was it because of their stance on the draft or on Vietnam? Or was it because they did not publish enough? Because the rules of the UC system are that you are granted tenure and advancement based on how much you publish. Well, some of the professors who were involved in all of these other wonderful activities that I have tried to describe were not publishing as much. And so for various reasons, Paul Lee was not granted tenure, and then Page Smith, who was the Provost of Cowell College, is reported to have said, "If this place (UCSC) does not have a place for Paul Lee, then it doesn't have a place for Page Smith."

So they both left the University along with some of the other faculty, and they moved down into town. I would say that all of that happened around 1974. Now some people would say that was the end of the golden days, those early days of UCSC, but I would actually contend that once they went down into town, wonderful new things happened. So it was like a kind of transformation. When they moved into town, between Page and Paul and the others, they started the William James Association, and in that, or out of that, they started things like the William James Work Company; it was sort of like a little Santa Cruz CCC project. They also started the Penny University, and it still goes on today. They started Paideia University as well.

Page Smith was really discontent with what had happened

to the PhD studies programs on campus and in higher education, where students had to become so very specialized and abstracted from broader aspects of life in their academic pursuits (as explained in his book *Killing the Spirit, Higher Education in America.*) He supported the Paideia idea that if you are going to give a PhD, the candidate should be a good scholar but also do something useful for the community as part of his academic achievement. That was going back to the ideal of Athens, Greece, where you were granted recognition for your academic work if you also, as part of your studies, did something useful with it for the community. And so that's where I got involved in Paideia with Page and we started working on the restoration of the San Lorenzo River. Also, the Homeless Garden Project grew out of that movement off campus. The Prison Arts Project that still goes on was the result of Eloise, Page's wife, getting involved in that project. And as I mentioned, a lot of things happened with the restoration of the lower San Lorenzo River, which ultimately resulted in the restoration plan and project that we do have in place now, and a lot of improvement along the lower part of the San Lorenzo River.

One of the other spin-offs that happened, was that KUSP Radio was started out of some of the same musical, social energy for the festivals that were going on. Also, another thing happened to me when I was asked not to return to UCSC Extension after the Earth Day celebration: my wife was pregnant at the time. We had been thinking about having a home birth. Shall we have a home birth or not, you know? At that time there were the beginnings of the midwife movement here in Santa Cruz. At the moon festivals there were a lot of women involved and some of them had had home births. Women and men were involved with playing music, dancing, sharing food. When I got laid off, we did not have any health insurance or income for awhile, and it became increasingly attractive to have a home birth. So we got involved in the home birth movement. There were home births going on in the community, and Mike can tell you about this over where he lived in Aptos, and so we had a home birth — and out of that, the whole midwife movement started becoming more active, and eventually there was a group of women who started the Center for the Feminine Arts and Midwifery up at Camp Campbell in Boulder Creek. So that was the beginning of the women's home birth movement, at least from our perspective.

A lot of new things happened, of course, politically. There were struggles over land use, energy use, the greenbelt idea, the lighthouse field battle, the battle over the atomic energy plant out in Davenport — all those things went on, but they happened in a way that was different because of the movement of activists from the campus into the community.

So I could go on and tell you stories for quite a long time, but I just wanted to say that, when I think about the early days at UCSC, I think not only of what happened up here on campus, but what happened to the whole community, and to these, what we call, alternative lifestyles, alternative energy, alternative cultural movements that started in the Santa Cruz Mountains. I think that this is what Callenbach picked up on and incorporated into his Ecotopian novels in various ways; not just what happened up here at UCSC, which was a little like a Utopia, but what happened in the whole community. And when we think about the future, what I see is that out of all this, it may seem like we have a duality. But there's really a potential for reintegration of all the wonderful things that have gone on, and are going on in the community, with all the positive things that have continued to happen up here at UCSC. And what I think is going to happen is that we're going to have an unintended Ecotopia.

Because of the challenges of global climate change, we have no other choice. If we're going to confront the real challenges that scientists tell us exist — that of not increasing the temperature more than 1.5 to 2 degrees centigrade, and bringing the carbon parts per million down to about 350 — we have to really implement huge technological lifestyle changes, and very, very fast. lI would say that lots of things that were prophesized in the Ecotopian novels will come to pass, because we have to make those changes soon, and we have to make them in a really massive, world-wide way.

So that's my hope for the future, and it was a joy to be able to share a little bit about my memories of the past, and my perspective.

7. Paul Lee

Paul wrote this story for the website. It was posted November 26, 2005.

Oceans of Desire Santa Cruz in the 1960s

"How could I fail to be grateful to my whole life? — and I tell my life to myself." Nietzsche: Ecce Homo

Bumping into a friend at the Harvard Coop who told me he had applied for a position at Santa Cruz but had changed his mind, I said, "Well, maybe I'll apply." He looked at me askance and said: "Do you know anything about the California University sssssystem?" I didn't, but I registered the hiss in the way he pronounced the word system. I thought: snake in the grass? I was teaching at M.I.T. and my term was about to expire and I needed a job. Soon after an article appeared in the New York Times that Kenneth Thimann had been appointed Provost of Crown College, UCSC. I went to the phone. I was a Fellow of a Radcliffe House where Thimann was Provost and I knew him. He was a very distinguished professor of botany at Harvard. We went over for tea and he hired me. Richard Baker, the eventual Zentatsu Myoyu and Zen Roshi, called, looking for Tillich and Erikson to invite to a conference he was organizing at Asilomar. I had been Tillich's Teaching Assistant and Erikson was my thesis advisor. They weren't available so I offered myself and he bought it, including my wife, so we flew out and got a look at Santa Cruz before moving there.

Driving down Pacific Ave. in 1965 was like driving down the main street in Paducah, in 1937, although I had never been there. It looked impossibly dull and old-fashioned. There was a men's clothing store that looked like used Sears. Definitely unhip. And then – stop the car! – the Hip Pocket Bookstore and over the door a Ron Boise sculpture from the Kama Sutra, a couple in a position, in flagrante delicto. Definitely hip! I double-parked and ran in to take a look and picked up a copy of the Black Mountain something or other, an underground newspaper, edited by Claire somebody. It was an island in the forth-coming "ocean of desire".

We met the Bakers at Asilomar and over drinks found out they were practicing Zen Buddhists. I didn't know any up to then, although I had attended a seminar given by Tillich and Hisamatsu, at Harvard. Hisamatsu, a famous Zen Master, was in residence at Harvard. I hardly understood a word, but he was interesting to observe and made a pronounced impression. I was intrigued by the challenge of an American taking on an Asian religion – an experiment in the cross-fertilization of cultures, or mind and migration, the title of an essay Tillich had written about the affinity of the mind for the migratory impulse. Here was a living instance, my new-found friends. I decided to appoint myself as Baker's protestant theological witness.

As I was a member of the Leary Group at Harvard and a founding editor of the *Psychedelic Review,* I told Baker, who was organizing conferences and symposia for the University Extension, he should do one on LSD, as it was going to become a big deal. He did. Berkeley tried to cancel it after they woke up to the hot potato and Baker had to compromise by moving the venue to the San Francisco campus and disinviting Allen Ginsberg, who showed up anyhow but did not appear on the program.

So a month or so before we moved to Santa Cruz, in 1966, I gave the opening address at the notorious LSD Conference in San Francisco. The conference was scheduled for a week which meant lots of time for parties and lots of fun. I thought of it as my reception to taking up residence for a new life in California. The first stop was the Psychedelic Bookstore in the Haight. Then on to the party thrown by the Grateful Dead in Marin with Owsley handing out his homemade acid to everyone who wanted it. It was a hoot. Hundreds of people on a big estate, almost all of them naked, swimming and passing joints rolled in newspapers. I had never seen anything like that before. I was there with Nina Graboi, whom we picked up at Alan Watts' houseboat in Sausalito, and she wrote up the event in her book on the '60's. I wasn't clear about what I was going to speak about so I decided to describe the party as the wave of the future and called my talk: "Psychedelic Style." I had never seen freaks before and there were a lot of them. We wore button down shirts and Brooks Brothers suits and thought we were running the show from Harvard. We were wrong and stood corrected. At one point a guy came out and announced that everyone had to move their cars as the neighbors had complained and they didn't want the cops to come. There were a lot of cars and everyone was stoned. An elephant seal like groan went up from the group. I thought, o.k., this is a test. If it happens without mishap it bodes well for the movement. It did. I felt hopeful. The Dead came out and played. A guy stood with his head inside one of the huge speakers and I asked. "Who is that?" Neal Cassady, I was told.

The week long conference was great – Rolf and Elsa Von Eckartsberg, Ralph Metzner, Leary, Huston Smith, our gang from Harvard, and Gerd Stern, and a host of others working in the psychedelic vineyard, took their turn. We had a party every night and Owsley hung around because someone had taken his dealer customer list by mistake in a purse exchange. He finally recovered it. When we met he was wearing a powder blue jump suit and looked up at me and said in a slightly blurred drawl: "My you have a friendly and familiar face!"

Someone fresh from down south gave me a joint of Panama Red as a present and the Von Eckartsbergs and my wife and I drove down to Santa Cruz, rented the wedding suite at the then Dream Inn, lit up and watched Herman and the Hermits on Ed Sullivan. After I scraped myself off the wall, we went out and rode the roller coaster and thought we were goners, pitched out over Monterey Bay, although we landed instead at Manuel's Restaurant at Seacliff Beach. Oh boy! Chicken mole and red snapper. We talked about the Conference and there was Claire from the Hip Pocket Bookstore with John Lingemann at the next table and he was straining every nerve to hear every word and finally unable to restrain himself came over and introduced himself and could hardly believe his good fortune at meeting a psychedelic philosopher and a psychedelic existential phenomenological psychologist who had taken acid at Harvard and were founding editors of the *Psychedelic Review*. John was a psychedelic well digger and a witcher, given his ability to locate water. Of German ancestry, he was a rude force. He eventually bulldozed his house from which his wife fled and ended up living in a cave on the property with a young woman. He offered to take us around and show us Santa Cruz the next day and we took him up on it. Some intro.

We had to go back to our summer home in Northern Wisconsin to collect our things and our daughter and drive back, so we did. After a week in motels, a different one every night, as I had some kind of phobic reaction to the smell, we finally landed in Rio del Mar, at Hidden Beach, just off the ocean. It was paradise. I stood on the deck and listened to the roar of the surf and wondered how long it would take to get used to it.

We met some of the early Heads in the area: Zoo, who was a wild Irish mover and had Superman painted on his truck, aka Gary Dunne, Tox, without the vobiscum, and Charlie Nothing, whose wedding to Carol Cole, one of Nat's daughters, my sister-in-law had attended in Los Angeles. They were complete nuts and had formed a group called Eternity, partly because it seemed like that long before they stopped playing. They had Ron Boise's Thunder Machine as their lead instrument and they performed at an ice cream store next to Shoppers' Corner. They always took acid and so they played for at least eight hours. I neglected to take it in. I never went to the Barn, either, the main psychedelic venue in the area.

They went down to Esalen as often as they could where they acted like the house band for the employees who liked getting stoned at night after work and going crazy until the wee hours, jumping across bonfires in an orgy of psychedelic bravado. I had occasion to witness this when I gave a seminar with Alan Watts on the future of consciousness. It didn't look good, but it was lots of fun. One night in the baths two mountain men hippies who had gone native living in the woods for some years stumbled in on their first night out and wanted to know who was President and what had happened in the world in their absence.

Everyone in the baths laughed out loud.

The Eternity boys ended up living at Lingemann's in the trees. They came down one night and tracked mud into my house and laughed derisively and poked fun at my Buddha, a Siamese Walking Buddha, a beautiful bronze sculpture. I never liked them after that.

I assumed my teaching duties. Santa Cruz was a hotbed for psychedelics and the university was thought of as a country club retreat in the redwoods where students could turn on. Dealers, so I was told, went up and down the corridors of the dormitories on Saturday, hawking their wares. Like Alice's Restaurant, you could get anything you wanted. I thought of an apt metaphor for the students: oceans of desire. The place had a way of releasing this particular longing, this surplus desire, a Marxist concept I should look up on google, but one that seemed to fit as there was definitely a lot of it. I remember going to Berkeley where there was even a greater buzz in the air than in Santa Cruz, and noticing a phenomenon I called the psychedelic eye. When you made eye contact with someone passing in the street there was an unspoken helllooooo and a goodbyeeeeee....as if time had stopped and the eternal now had had its moment. Ships in the night in broadest daylight. The ache of longing, the desire to get it on, the interest in chance encounters and willingness to risk it, seize the moment, all in a glance – it was that kind of a time.

We had arrived in Santa Cruz just after the demise of the Sticky Wicket, a local watering hole where everyone hung out. We found out that Manuel Santana, who was a remarkably talented artist as well as a restauranteur, and Al Johnsen, a local potter, had organized the art scene in town. I bought a piece by Tony Magee and a construction piece by Joe Lysowski, a chair, a table, a pair of skis and a painting, in a fabulous psychedelic style. I still have the group minus the painting.

We started making pilgrimages to San Francisco at least once a month to visit the Bakers and catch the action. Quicksilver Messenger Service was my favorite group. The first Be-in took place. Leary was there, the guest of honor, and so was Suzuki-roshi. We had a picnic on the grass and everyone was mellow on grass. The tribe had gathered. I took slides. Afterward we went to Margot Doss' for dinner with Leary who was flushed with excitement over the day. Margot wrote a popular column on walking in the Bay area for the San Francisco Chronicle. She fixed up Tim with a lovely young thing who was in a trance state over the encounter. Margot had a mound of crab on a buffet that was eye boggling. A mountain of fresh crab, the delicacy of the area; more than anyone could possibly eat.

I was invited to give a talk on the Be-in by my first Santa Cruz friend, the Rev. Herb Schmidt, whom my wife and I had met on our Asilomar trip. He met us at the front door wearing a black bikini and holding a martini. I thought, this is my kind of Lutheran. He set it up as a debate with the Assistant Chief of Police, Officer Overton, a big mistake. I showed my slides thinking they would educate the group to the new style of life and what to expect from the younger generation. They were appalled. They thought Overton should cuff me and take me away before I was lynched. Fortunately, I lived a block away and figured I could make a run for it if I could only get out the door. A young Sunday school teacher stood up and berated the group for their ill will toward me and started to weep which further alerted me to my peril. That settled things down a bit and I got home safely. The experience didn't make me any more cautious and I continued to speak publicly about psychedelics, thinking I was carrying on my duties as an educator. I went to Rice University and spoke and met Rusty Schweikert, the astronaut, who was on his way into outer space without the use of drugs. I met Danny Lyon, the photographer, who was doing a shoot on the Texas penitentiary system and had met one of the symbolic prisoners in the country, Billy McKuen, who had cut his penis off in prison; we carried on a correspondence.

I was critical of the psychedelic movement after it became clear that there were casualties to take into account. Students who never recovered from a bad trip became a new type of social welfare recipient – crippled for life, they went on the dole. I talked about the tyranny of being hip and the pressure to take

drugs although it deterred no one. I was worried about defor-
mation, about the de-structuring of consciousness that occurred
under the influence of the drug, often associated with a death
experience. from which some experimenters never recovered.
They were permanently de-structured and found it impossible
to return to what they had been if you want to call that normal.
They became wards of the State. I met one of the casualties
out on the road in front of Stevenson College. I remember the
moment vividly – a former student, Tom somebody, who, for a
year or more had been living on the beaches and probably in a
cave and whose eyes flashed like a movie projector gone haywire,
you could almost hear the sound of the film flapping off the reel.

I understood the yearning of the spirit and the desire to form
an opposition movement against the socially dominant estrange-
ment – Leary summed it up in the slogan of the time: Turn on,
tune in, and drop out. "She's leaving home......" the Beatles
sang. This inner emigration swept through the younger generation like a wave and they disengaged psychically from the
collective insanity that was going on around them, learning how
to hide in public view. I was fascinated by this covert ethic, as
I called it, exemplified by watching students in a circle, say, at
a wedding, or some social gathering, passing a joint and taking a toke as if no one noticed. An invisible line separated the
straights from the hip. It was clear that this freedom of the
spirit was indistinguishable from arbitrary willfulness.

It became apparent to me that there were certain users who
lived to light up. They were constantly looking for the moment
when they could get stoned; all other experience, including time
spent with one another, was subordinate to their central and
all-consuming obsession; they were addicts. It was a matter
of observation to watch them bide their time and to give off
the impression that at any given moment they could repeat the
ritual they lived for: to light up! They seemed to be entirely
oblivious that this was the case and that an observer such as
myself could call them to account. The reason for doing so was
because one had the feeling of being used – manipulated – for
the purpose of collusion in the assumed mutually shared interest

in getting stoned. There was a perceived psychic drumming of fingers and an imperceptible hum to mark the time.

It reminded me of visiting relatives in Norway who put on a Sunday afternoon spread for a prince. Plums in clotted cream and aquavit, the national drink, which entailed a ritual. Everyone raises their glass and says skol, looks one another in the eye, clinks glasses and bottoms up. Refill. Wait. Small talk. Some quiet drumming of fingers and a little humming. And then someone breaks the suspense when the appropriate time has passed and says skol and the ritual is repeated. Needless to say, as this goes on, the intervals get shorter and shorter and the sham of waiting becomes more and more transparent and provokes great hilarity. It was the Norwegian version of stoned.

I taught at Cowell College the first year before I moved to Crown. Page Smith had hired me, accommodating me until Crown opened. We became great friends, as well as his wife, Eloise. They were the spirit of the place and imbued Cowell with a charm and culture that was stunning and unforgettable. I met Mary Holmes and we fell in love on the spot, the beginning of a lifelong friendship. And then came Chadwick.

I have had a few clairvoyant experiences in my life but this was one of the best. Maybe clairvoyant isn't the word. It was more like being guided. I thought a student garden project would be a good thing for the campus, even though I wasn't interested in gardening and didn't know where the idea came from; although, after all, the campus was on a splendid ranch landscape, the weather was perfect, and "Flower Power" was in the air, another slogan of the times, wafting down on a cloud of smoke from the Haight. We all got a whiff of that. So I asked the Chancellor to lead a walk to look for a prospective site. He thought it was a good idea. Quite a few people showed up and I carried my daughter on my shoulders and we looked around up behind Crown where there were running streams and gorgeous stands of redwoods, eucalyptus and oak.

Two weeks later, Chadwick arrived. I was told of his coming by Countess Freya von Moltke, who was visiting the campus and had heard of my project. She said she had my gardener for me. I met Chadwick at the Cowell Fountain and asked him if he would take on the task and he said he would. The next day he went out and bought a spade and picked out the slope below Merrill College and started to dig. I remember driving up to school and catching him out of the corner of my eye and thinking, Oh boy, here we go! I think it was the first organic garden at a university in the country. 1967.

We were right in line for Earth Day, three years later, as if the garden had been planned as a place to celebrate it. The garden jeopardized my career, although not publishing was another factor. I thought the garden would count as a bad book but I was wrong. And it didn't help that I was the founding chair of religious studies and my field was the philosophy of religion. My colleagues at Crown gave me the thumbs down. The handwriting on the wall appeared fairly early. After the suicide of a colleague, I thought the message was clear. I was finished. So I dreamt up a nonprofit corporation as a pipe dream that might afford me a place to work – I called it U.S.A., University Services Agency. Three days after the new year – 1970 – I ran into my pal, Herb Schmidt, who was campus chaplain, as he was about to get the franchise for the only public restaurant on the campus and I proposed my idea. The non-profit took off like a rocket. We started the Whole Earth Restaurant and Sharon Cadwallader took on the task and her cookbook sold a million copies. Eventually we had something like thirty affiliates and millions in cashflow. I thought of writing it up as: How To Become A Spiritual Millionaire When Money Is No Object. It anticipated Page Smith and me starting the William James Association, after I was bounced. When Page retired in protest over the issue, he said: "any place that doesn't have room for Paul Lee doesn't have room for me." Even today it has a nice ring.

The Loyalty Oath was an attempt to break the spirit of American intellectuals and one was practically forced to sign it in order to get paid. University professors were suspect in principle. It was a test of one's mettle – what I call thymic juice or the ability to say No! *(Thymos* is the ancient Greek word for

courage.) It takes courage to resist and the willingness to accept
the penalty for noncompliance with evil which is Gandhi's definition of satyagraha, his term for the moral equivalent of war.
There was a penalty to pay either way: might as well come out
with one's integrity intact. I witnessed the courage of colleagues
at M.I.T., when I saw them take a stand and refuse to sign. I
didn't have to sign because I was on my way to Santa Cruz.
I knew Erik Erikson at Harvard and I knew he had refused to
sign at Berkeley and was forced to leave his position. He told me
they had an office for the purpose that was open 24 hours a day
so faculty could sneak in at three in the morning undetected.
I admired him for his courage but I signed. I was ashamed of
myself because I transgressed a scruple against swearing my true
faith and allegiance to the constitution of the State of California. Allegiance, sure, but true faith? That was reserved for
more transcendent swearing. I went to Santa Barbara to be on
a panel. The lady in charge offered me a piece of paper to sign
after I finished speaking. I asked what it was and she said the
Loyalty Oath. I told her I had signed it. She said it didn't matter. I had to sign every time I spoke at another campus in order
for them to pay me. I handed the paper back. No thanks. Keep
your honorarium. Years later, the Loyalty Oath was overturned
and I called Santa Barbara and they sent the check. No interest.
I realized I had lost and won a round with myself. How many
rounds does one get?

I remember the first time I saw Ralph Abraham. It was at
a Faculty meeting in the fall of 1968. He was sitting in the
front row. I did a doubletake as I walked by. I thought holy
shit, they hired Abbie Hoffman; now they've gone too far! We
were asked to lead a student protest against the regents who
were making a visit to the campus. Reagan was governor. The
Democratic convention police riot in Chicago had happened a
few months before and the campus was a tinder box ready to
explode. Ronnie and the regents were the match.

I arrived for the march wearing my Harvard PhD robe, red
silk with black bands, a representative of lawful order and adult
circumspection; Ralph showed up wearing an American flag

shirt. We both had beards and Ralph had an afro out to there. The students for the most part behaved but there were some outside agitators from Berkeley who acted as provocateurs and wanted to foment trouble. I invited the biggest loudmouth out into the parking lot but he declined.

Bill Moore, who was to become a graduate student in the History of Consciousness Program, had called for a Black Studies College in honor of Malcolm X and the Chancellor, McHenry, had laughed derisively at the suggestion. Bill was considered an inside agitator and was persona non grata for making speeches on the campus. In the middle of the ruckus he was removed from the campus by the police. I found out about it and picked him up at the bottom of the campus where he had been deposited and brought him back, where we were met by student supporters with whom we locked arms and marched into the Crown College courtyard. There, we were met by Rich Townsend, a student sympathetic to Moore's proposal, who told us that Jesse Unruh and a number of regents were waiting to talk to Bill. In we went to the Crown Library and Bill sat down to repeat his proposal, this time to sympathetic ears. Eventually, the X in Malcolm X was transposed to Oakes and a college devoted to Black Studies was instituted.

Ralph's and my picture appeared in many of the state newspapers in articles about the demonstration. Hate mail poured in. People didn't like professors with beards and they really didn't like their flag worn as a shirt. McHenry dutifully sent copies to us with a little red check on a tab on the side of the document. One of them suggested we fill our pockets with shit and lie down in front of a bus and become instantly embalmed. I thought that was an example of a rare imagination. Ralph had tenure and I didn't. I thought the jig was up for me and it turned out to be true, even though the Crown faculty gave me a vote of confidence at the time which was really a veiled kiss of death.

A Vietnam Teach-in was organized and many of us spoke, including John Kroyer, my colleague in philosophy, who recommended that students hand back their draft cards; after all it was government property, let the government take care of it. The Chancellor took umbrage at the event and especially Kroyer's remarks and proceeded to censure him which meant his advancement was jeopardized. It precipitated a nervous breakdown not helped by a bad mescaline trip and I had to have him institutionalized. He was eventually released after shock treatment and bought a gun and shot himself. I thought it was a message sent to me that I was dead as far as my teaching career was concerned. I had to conduct his funeral service. I quoted Dylan Thomas:*oh you who could not cry on to the ground, now break a giant tear, for this little known fall.*

McHenry eventually went after Ralph Abraham. McHenry was an ex-marine, which explains something. Steno pool wastepaper baskets were raided for incriminating evidence. Are you kidding? Charges were trumped up. Ralph decided to write to all the major mathematicians in the world to complain. He was fed up. The day after they got the letters McHenry called it off. Chalk up one round for the good guys.

I started to get critical of the institution, remembering the hissed 's' and appalled at McHenry's repressive behavior. I thought of three things haunting higher education: the triumph of the obtuse, the bureaucratization of the learning process and the principle of anonymity, where students would never find roots or a place to nurture them. And I could tell that the first five years, from 1965 to 1970, when the humanities counted, would soon be swept away or at least under the carpet by the triumph of the sciences. We were enjoying what was only a brief grace period. Short but sweet. It always surprised me that for Page Smith this was enough. That it had had it's time at all seemed to be a matter of unassailable affirmation for him. Sometimes brief flowerings of the spirit are better than no flowerings at all.

Page did have second thoughts about it, though. Late in life he wrote a blistering indictment of the university system entitled: *Killing the Spirit,* his critique of the deadening force of reductionism that had descended on higher education like a pall, with the message that only the sciences counted for knowledge and all the rest was a waste of time to be reluctantly tolerated. To pay homage to the book and the critique I wanted to install a spiritual cloakroom at the entrance to the campus in front of the sign bearing the school slogan: *Fiat lux*. Incoming students would check their spirits for safekeeping and I would give them a number and when they graduated it would be returned to them if we could find it. It didn't surprise me at all when the former chancellor, M.R.C. Greenwood consistently referred to the university as a major research institution and not a university.

I decided to teach a course that would critically examine the university. I called it "Organizational Climate," a term developed by a former colleague at Harvard Business School. I thought the students should study the institution they were enrolled in and not take it for granted. I organized the class as a non-profit corporation, as I was enamored of the form, and issued stock. We took on some interesting projects, the first having to do with a seasonal erosion of a hillside at the entrance to the campus where the soil spilled down onto the road every winter in the rainy season. There was a dispute between the county and the university over jurisdiction and responsibility. The class met in the only geodesic dome on the campus, and we called in the appropriate authorities and interrogated them and the dispute was resolved. Then we decided to build a retaining wall in front of the Chadwick Garden as it was also eroding in the rains. We got the stone from the quarry on the campus and a crew turned out and we did a nice job. I got a nasty letter sent to me with a copy to the chancellor from Building and Grounds disavowing any responsibility for the wall and its tumbling down in the first rain. It's still there.

One student said she wanted to make bread and give it away. I said ok. She wanted some money so I gave her some and she obtained the kitchen at the Congregational Church on High Street. Her name was Bonny. She was famous for taking acid in high school and taking her clothes off before she was arrested. I forget how many loaves she baked. That summer, while we were in Wisconsin, I got a letter from her saying this guy is hitchhiking out to see me and wants to borrow some money to start a bakery. He had the ovens but he needed money for flour. I winced. Days later I get a call from Eagle River, a town ten miles away. He's here.

I drove in to pick him up. He doesn't talk. We sit on the back porch steps for a few days enjoying the quiet and I finally mention I will take him back to the phone booth in Eagle River and he can hitchhike back. He didn't say a word. Shortly after, I get word that my colleague, John Kroyer, had shot himself and I was asked to return to perform his funeral service. I was so down I looked up the baker and there he was in a little hole in the wall on Seabright and Murray, sitting on his oven. I gave him the rent I was collecting on our home so he could buy flour. He got started and eventually sold it and it became the Staff of Life Bakery. I never got my money back, just like my rent for the Bookshop Santa Cruz. I should have gone to Harvard Business School instead of Harvard Divinity School. But I developed a pained appreciation for an economy of gift and the application of Erik Erikson's definition of identity: you have it to give it away!

One day after an Organizational Climate class, a coed came up and said she was going home to visit her grandmother. I was a little perplexed but I said say hello to her for me. She came back after the break and handed me a check for ten grand. I said who's your grandmother? Mrs. J. C. Penney. So we designed a project for the summer. A group from the class would spend the summer with Ron Bevirt, aka Hassler, a former Merry Prankster, who lived on Last Chance Road. They had a ball. I was a little concerned about accountability so I asked Hassler to write up the project. He handed in a very nice document of about 25 pages entitled: "No Holes Barred Finishing School, The Same Eastern Polish at a Fraction of the Cost."

A student got caught in an elevator malfunction with Ken Kesey in San Francisco. For some hours. I guess it was a life-transforming experience. She came into my office and wanted me to agree that she should drop out of school. I agreed. Then she fell in love with Hassler and wanted me to marry them. I agreed and we performed the ceremony at the Sacred Oak in the middle of Pogonip. My daughter, Jessica, was the bridesmaid.

I had a horse that I kept on campus. His name was Charley when I bought him and I renamed him Xanthos, the horse of Achilles, who prophesied Achilles' death. I thought it was a good name for a philosopher's horse. I had gone riding with Mary Holmes and she said why don't I get a horse. I almost fell off. I had wanted to be a cowboy in the summer and a fireman in the winter when I was a boy. I never thought I would fulfill one of them. She found a quarter horse gelding, a magnificent specimen. I was in seventh heaven, another name for the saddle. I had to move him eventually and found a stable up on Spring Street at Windy Hill Farm with a lady who had run polo ponies at Pogonip.

I could get on to the Pogonip across the road and it afforded me 614 acres of prime riding space. One day while doing a turn in a meadow I looked up at the solitary oak standing in the middle and saw the Crucified. The oak tree was in the form of the Crucified, a major limb had broken off leaving a head. The outstretched limbs below looked like arms. It was the place name – Santa Cruz, Holy Cross – in an oak. I started having services there on Thanksgiving, Christmas and Easter. The year was 1977. Pogonip was threatened with development by the Cowell Foundation and I thought: over my dead body. I started the Save Pogonip Greenbelt Group with Mark Primack and he drew the oak for the poster and we passed an initiative that lead to the city acquiring the property as a park. I continue to do services there with my colleague, Herb Schmidt.

In 1970, I met Jack Stauffacher, of the Greenwood Press, in San Francisco, one of the great fine press typographers in the world. He was a devotee of Goethe and when he found out we had a Goethean Gardener in Alan Chadwick, he wanted to meet him.

Alan practiced biodynamics, a form of horticulture developed by Rudolf Steiner in the early part of the last century. Steiner was a Goethean and took much of his inspiration from Goethe, particularly Goethe's botany. We had adopted the slogan of Goethe's Italian Journey:*Et in Arcadia Ego,* for our gar-

den. Arcadia is the garden theme of Greek letters, comparable to
Eden. Virgil's Georgics is the classic text. Jack did a broadside
devoted to the theme, commemorating the garden. We formed
a lifelong friendship and eventually he did a fine press edition of
Plato's *Phaedrus* and dedicated it to me.

I nominated Jack for a Regents' Professorship and he came
to Cowell College and started the Cowell Press. He had a distinguished group of students, some of whom went into fine printing
and have had great careers. I gave a talk at Holy Cross Church
on Goethe's *Italian Journey* on the occasion of the 200th anniversary and Jack did an exquisite broadside for the occasion.

When Page Smith and I left the university in 1972, we started
the William James Association. Page wanted to start the Civilian Conservation Corps over again as he had been in a leadership training camp in Norwich, Vermont, in 1940, inspired by
William James' address at Stanford in 1906: "A Moral Equivalent of War." It involved his beloved teacher – Rosenstock
Huessy – to whom he was devoted for the rest of his life and
it was an experience he never got over. It was something like an
unpaid debt as the camp was shortlived due to the war and Page
was drafted. So we went to Washington, D. C., but we didn't
get anywhere. Then Eloise asked me to ask Baker-roshi to ask
Gov. Brown to nominate her as the Chair of the State Arts
Council, about to be newly formed. She knew I was friends
with Baker-roshi and he was a friend of Brown and so I did.
When she and Page were in Brown's office in Sacramento to be
named he gave the State of the State Address and announced
the forthcoming California Conservation Corps. Page jumped
in his seat and told Brown about our work to that end at the
national level. Brown said, "be my guest" and so we got to do
the early planning for the corps. That was a coincidence of an
unusual sort. Makes one wonder.

After some months, this guy appears in our office in Santa
Cruz, and introduces himself as the new director of the Corps
– Boyd Horner. I asked him what he had done before. He had
studied for the Rudolf Steiner Priesthood in England. I said,
Oh go on, your're just shitting me. In fact, I looked up my

sleeve thinking something strange and weird had crawled out.
He proceeded to make the Corps a Rudolf Steiner Corps. God
wot! He was the moonbeam in the Governor's office. I was
sent to England to the Steiner School there – Emerson College.
He wanted Steiner gymnasts, Steiner dieticians, Steiner dancers
(Eurythmy), and probably Steiner geometers. Anything Steiner
I could get. I went into a pub in Forest Row and they could tell
I was from California. When I told them I was visiting Emerson,
they ducked, and I thought a bat had flown in thru the window.
The Steiner group was pretty weird. I had fun going into London
on weekends and hanging out with Harrison Ford, my brother-
in-law, who was acting in Star Wars. We drank single malt
scotch. McCallums. I got to go to the set and watch him being
made up and thought his uniform was the dickiest thing I had
ever seen, like they had made it out of old handkerchiefs. I
thought, this thing is never going to fly.

Horner didn't last long and that was the end of that as far
as our relation to the Corps was concerned.

I thought land reform was going to be the next big thing after
civil rights. I organized a conference at the Civic Auditorium.
There was a guy running for the presidency on a land reform
plank, his name escapes me. I was his local campaign manager.
Harris. His name was Harris. There was Riis Tijerina, who was
a Southwestern radical and had staged a demonstration in favor
of minority rights. And there was Cesar Chavez. I thought they
were continuing the tradition of a moral equivalent of war.

No one came. Fortunately, I had invited about forty speakers. They made for a small audience and talked to themselves.
Stauffacher did a broadside. I was not only ahead of my time, I
was out of my time. But it did lead to my starting the Northern
California Land Trust, with Erich Hansch and Warren Webber,
an organic farmer in Marin, who just hosted the Prince of Wales.
The idea of a land trust had just come to me as the vehicle for
land reform and land conservation and someone said there was a
guy who had just moved to Santa Cruz and had written a book
on how to do it. Take me to him. It was Erich. He was living
in a garage with Don Newey. I remember the shirts and pants

on hangers on a pole. Erich was a follower of Steiner. He was
an Anthroposophist. Really, the coincidences were piling up. I
thought this makes up for a lot. Erich was wonderful and I loved
him dearly. He reminded me of my grandfather in Milwaukee
who was into the occult.

Migrating hippies wandering through Santa Cruz became
known as the Undesirable Transient Element or "Ute's". Some
inspired local bureaucrat must have made up that one. One of
the first things Page and I did in the William James Association
was to organize the Work Company so that the transients could
find short term, part time, employment. We found 30,000 jobs
during the life of the project. Not bad. We started a Community Garden project with Rock Pfotenhauer. Page and Eloise
started the Prison Arts Project, which had remarkable success
and became a national model. And then we got involved with
the homeless in 1985 and opened the first public shelter in Santa
Cruz, and then the homeless church program, with churches taking in the overflow, and then the Homeless Garden Project and
then the Page Smith Community House. But that takes us out
of the 60's and 70's.

I almost forgot about the Wild Thyme Restaurant. That
was in the 70's. Max Walden had developed Cooper House from
the old County Court House and made it into the center of
downtown life. Bob Page and Ed Gaines and I opened the first
shop in the Cooper House – The Wilderness Store. The first one
in Santa Cruz. We even got the first Levi Franchise. Max had
a series of failed restaurants in the basement and so I offered
to start one. I was enamoured of the herb thyme because of
the Greek root – thymos – my favorite word and the herb was
thymus vulgaris in the Latin, derived from the Greek. So was the
thymus gland, the master organ of the immune system. So we
served sweetbreads which are calve thymus glands, the supreme
achievement of French cuisine – Joanne LeBoeuf was the chef
and had a knack with the glands; and hamburgers with thyme,
which made people protest because they thought it was pork,
so I got laughed at. I went around and lectured people on their
thymus glands; remember this was early, so almost no one knew

they had one, and once I had their attention, lectured them on the physicalist/vitalist conflict in the system of the sciences as a rap on the late stage of the self-destruction of industrial society. I had a cue card that gave the bullets so you could get the main points at a glance.

Buckminster Fuller came in one night with a student from the University. He said hello, Paul, which knocked me out as I had met him with a hundred other people at a reception in Los Gatos, months before. I was having a meeting in the back room of a group that was going to publish a journal as part of our Bicentennial Grant which Page and I had received for art projects for Santa Cruz. Page was the Bicentennial Historian, as the first two volumes of his History of the U.S. were to coincide with the Bicentennial. I asked Bucky if he would say a few words to the group and he was glad to oblige and charmed everyone with his remarks. He invited me to his table and I sat down. I thought this was my chance to ask him what he thought about Kurt Gödel and the incompleteness theorems and the undecidability problem. He never heard of Gödel. I was stunned but I proceeded to tell him what I knew, as the kid with him grew more and more agitated and kept saying, Bucky, do you realize the importance of what this man is saying? I enjoyed the response but he seemed a little over-heated. Finally, he ran out and I asked Bucky what was the deal and he said the kid had been raised at Synanon, the ex-drugee group, where his mother was in residence and he was rather hyper-active. Maybe I should check on him. I went to the front of the restaurant and there he was on the phone booking a plane for Princeton to see Gödel. He said he had a document in his pocket that was fraught with the greatest importance for mankind and he wanted to show it to Gödel. I asked him what it was and he wouldn't show it to me. Only Gödel. I was sorry I had told him.

I met Bucky once again at a conference where Chadwick was in residence. He came out of a portable potty standing in a field. It looked like he had just landed. He didn't remember me.

Jay Greenberg, a mathematician colleague at UCSC, had told me about Gödel around 1970. He told me that Gödel had written a proof for the existence of God. I saw stars. I thought if I could get the proof and publish it in a journal I was promoting for the History of Consciousness Program in order to fulfill the publish or perish demand that I knew they were going to get me on, I would be safe. I would get tenure on Gödel's Proof. Moreover, a proof by the world's leading mathematical logician would be irrefutable. I wrote to Gödel. He wrote back and said the proof was incomplete. Everyone laughed. I was waiting for Gödel. And, he asked, what did theology have to do with consciousness? That threw me for awhile. I had occasion to call him at Princeton when I told a friend of mine, Adelaide de Menil, to take a picture of him, as she was going to Princeton to visit her brother. Adelaide is a fine photographer. She said I had to set it up. Hello, Prof. Gödel. This is Prof. Lee. Remember me? Yes. I wrote to you about your proof. Is it complete? No. Oh, too bad. And when you asked about the relation of theology to consciousness, oh, never mind. Could I have a friend of mine come and take your picture? No. Why not? I have two perfectly good pictures of myself.

I had occasion to have coffee with Octavio Paz shortly after that and I told him the story about Gödel. He spilled his coffee in his lap. I thought that's how startled and excited a world-renowned poet gets when he hears that existence has become a predicate again. Kant said existence is not a predicate because it doesn't add anything conceptual to a thought. Existence is always assumed in the thinking of anything. At least conceptual existence. If you say that you have the thought of a hundred dollars and then that the hundred dollars exists, you can't find it in your pocket. So with that Kant undermined arguments for the existence of God. He thought it was like pulling a rabbit out of a hat. Since Kant, such arguments, which constitute a major theme in the history of philosophy have suffered in validity. Not after Gödel. Ha ha. And the proof is now complete and is to be found in the third volume of his collected papers. The only problem is it is completely unintelligible, at least to me and anyone else who is not a technically proficient mathematical logician. But I don't care. I still like the way it looks and am proud of having corresponded with Gödel and spoken to him on the phone even if it didn't save my ass.

So much for the 60's and 70's. They were fine while they lasted and I got my kicks on Route 66. Psychedelics were certainly the defining feature, and even though in many ways the 60's were a disappointment, psychedelics were terrific as a defining style. But it was thought to be more than that. It was hoped to be more than that. What happened to the longing that was released? The utopianism? It was nowhere, literally. And then it ended. They had a ceremony for it in the Haight. It was the death of the hippie. It had been co-opted by commercialism. Industrial society had absorbed it more than it was transformed by it or undermined by it. The opening of the doors of perception, the inter-modal sense quality experience, synesthesia, mystical flights, seeing the world in a flower, listening to Leary read from James Joyce, walking through a doorway, the revelatory power of a painting like when I discovered Cezanne at the Museum of Fine Arts in Chicago and my eyes were opened to his brush stroke and use of color, the symbiotic rapport and the sense of clairvoyance, Don Juan and Castaneda and the renewed appreciation of shamans, and all the gurus who filed through, many of them bogus and frauds, and then came that evil creep, Manson, and the Hells Angels beating to death an innocent bystander at a Rolling Stones concert.

Well, after all, what is marijuana, but an herb that burns.

Part V

The Catalyst, Fall 1966

8. Judy Hill

Judy wrote this story recently for this volume.

INTRODUCTION

Spring, 1966 — Self-catapulted from Berkeley in the midst of political activism after four years at a nearby art college. At first I was heavily involved in all the unrest, loving it in fact, then I got tired of the conflict, police everywhere, the increasing split between students and cops, bars over the windows of stores along Telegraph. A lot was changing, fast...our local beer hub, the Rathskeller, had been a lodestar for the Cal community, but the mood had shifted there and elsewhere, as the ballads of the Kingston Trio gave way first to Dylan and Baez, then to Hendrix, Morrison, Joplin, and others. Across the Bay, the Fillmore and Avalon Ballrooms were ramping up with what would turn out to be some of the greatest music of the 60s. While in school I had sat in the quad when Bob Dylan held forth; likewise, Joan Baez, Neal Cassady and others. None of them were luminaries yet...Dylan sat with a pouty face talking to a friend of mine. Cassady was speeding on some drug or another, motor-mouthing a mile a minute. I had grown up in this area, but everything about its current chaos unnerved me. I longed to get away from the noise, and planned to relocate to Santa Cruz as soon as school was out. My friends warned me that Santa Cruz was the "drug capital of the world." Who were they kidding? Drugs were everywhere, especially in Berkeley. I had been going down to Santa Cruz since I was a kid; the only thing I wanted was to live by the beach. And I wanted quiet.

Driving down 17 through the mountains was, at least at that time, a delight: very little traffic, the giant redwoods separating urbanity from vacation-time. I found my house by the beach; actually I found several. It's hard to believe now, but rentals were available everywhere. Neither UCSC nor San Jose (not yet named "Silicon Valley") were large enough to have any noticeable impact on housing or much of anything else. I ended

up renting a cute, semi-dilapidated, beach cottage three houses
up from Seabright (then known as Castle) Beach. My rent was
$55.00 a month, including utilities. When I left, my landlords
offered to sell me the property along with its adjacent huge lot,
for $17,000. I demurred, proud that I was an unencumbered free
spirit who could fit all her belongings into a backpack — one of
those decisions-you'll-regret-for-the-rest-of-your-life.

THE CATALYST

I assumed I'd be getting a waitress job somewhere; it was easy
to live here — many of my friends worked at restaurants in
some capacity, taking advantage of the rise in business during
the summer months, then collecting unemployment during the
winter. Also taking advantage of the free meal that generally
came with the job; a real perk since a high wage was $2.50 —
which gives a different slant on my rent. My best friend worked
at Manny's in Aptos, and that's where I wanted to be. My
boyfriend was into the flamenco scene there and Manny would
often join us at our table after-hours for spontaneous "juergas."
Manny's, the Sticky Wicket, and the Purple Cow were some of
the very few cool places to hang outside the immediate Santa
Cruz area. Instead, I got offered a job at the Shadowbrook
which, although beautiful then and now, catered to the very
prevalent conservative element; something I couldn't hack. Then
a friend told me about a new coffee house that was opening
downtown — the Catalyst. Downtown was dead back then;
lots of long-gone businesses with boarded up storefronts. Just
about the only thing alive was the Bookshop, Bubble Bakery,
Tampico, and Ford's department store. The whole area gave off
an "Invasion of the Bodysnatchers" vibe. Still stuck in the 50s,
the Del Mar and Rio were the only theaters in town, and they
showed the same movie day in and day out through the entire
summer.

Walking into the Catalyst the first time was like meeting
long-lost friends: Al and Patti DiLudovico had lived on a houseboat in Sausalito but had relocated to Santa Cruz to begin a new

chapter in their lives. Al was a huge huggy bear, with a great, wicked sense of humor; his wife Patti was the soft counterpart to Al's edge. Lots of people were put off by Al — his blunt, epithet-laden humor, his size, his face mostly hidden behind a full beard, his unforgiving attitude about bullshit of any kind, especially the version run by the freeloaders who started hanging out at the Catalyst as soon as it opened its doors. What they didn't know was the other side: the man who was a Quaker minister, who got up at 6 a.m. every morning to read his bible, or his commitment to helping the downtrodden. I loved both Al & Patti instantly. Another thing often forgotten at that time was that the Catalyst was a co-op, run by a group of investors looking for return on their investment. Al and Patti took a lot of shit for how they ran it, but most of the decisions were out of their hands. After working there for a while I got to know all the investors; some were involved because they thought the Catalyst had the potential to be a very cool place; others just wanted a return on the buck. Although Al and Patti were the face of the place, they were constantly getting pushed from behind.

When I first began working there, about a month after it opened, there was word that Mario Savio, on the lam from Berkeley police, was camping out in the basement. This was feasible: there was a huge network of caverns beneath these old buildings. But I thought: Please God, don't let the Berkeley madness come down here. And it didn't, not until years later, and at that time it was known as UCSC. The Catalyst was tiny when it opened — counter-service only with just a few tables up front. The deli was located in the small room facing Front Street — the Redwood Room, so named because of the split redwood bark panels on the walls. This stuff was immediately removed, probably because it caused welts on the skin of anyone who inadvertently brushed up against it. Later, the Fountain Room opened, and later still, the old ballroom. This was in the old St. George hotel, which still had residents — ancient residents, who would wander in for a cup of coffee, look around, and feel more lost than before. The place was falling apart, but it was startling beautiful even so. The Fountain Room had

Saltillo tile floors, mirrored walls, and an enormous fountain in the middle of the room with a large glass skylight several stories overhead, a skylight that funneled soft, muted light into this room in the center of a hotel; muted, because it had probably never been cleaned since the day it was installed. The Fountain Room was connected by a small walkway to the early Bookshop Santa Cruz, owned by Ron Lau, and next door, Aries Arts. These spaces were the former Hip Pocket Bookstore, and they were dark. Smoking weed was not loose the way it is now; in fact, it was severely punished at that time, so it wasn't really a surprise to stumble across someone lurking in that indoor alleyway, taking a furtive toke. Tucked off another side of the Fountain Room was the bar — a small, intimate cave with dark walnut interior and an amber glass ceiling. Because there was no money, of necessity Patti was the first bartender; later it was manned by Stan Fullerton, another huggy bear, this time a gruff one, who was an artist. Everyone in Santa Cruz thought of themselves as artists, but he actually was — a big, quiet guy, who never talked about himself and whose work I wanted badly to buy if only I could make enough money. He made Al seem almost diminutive. Stan was the ear for all the breakups, drug busts, and other problems of the day. He was silent for the most part, but served as a bouncer should the occasion arise; all it took was his presence and one look, and issues seemed to straighten themselves out. Eventually, the Catalyst expanded into the Colonial Room. This spectacular space had once been the St. George's ballroom, but for many decades had been humiliated into serving as storage for County Bank records. The good news was that due to lack of use the hardwood floors were pretty much intact, as were the walls, which were decorated with wood nymphs dancing among flowers and greenery. The deli was moved from the small front room and took up a full wall in the Colonial Room. I worked split shifts — at the deli during morning and lunch service; then at night when the mood shifted to table service. I loved this time at the old Catalyst. Every morning Al would open the enormous wall of windowed doors that swung open to Front Street. Patti would put on mellow music — the Art of the Psaltery, John Fahey, sometimes Vivaldi. Although acid-rock was everywhere, the Catalyst at that time was distinctly bohemian. A stage was set up for poetry, book readings, chamber music and acoustic guitar concerts. Patti had been a traveling ballad singer/guitarist before meeting Al, and occasionally she sat in with performers.

The Catalyst was the hub for downtown Santa Cruz, with a huge mix of people — the generation ahead of me, which included Al and Patti and people in their age group — the Beats; people my age or thereabouts, the so-called hippies; the "suits" — lawyers and admin from the county building across the river; and gaggles of kids from various communes. Everyone converged at the Catalyst. I think it's safe to say that everyone who lived here during that time, and many of those who traveled through, stopped by for a cup of 25-cent, free-refills coffee, New York-deli-style food, or just to check out the scene. The place lost money, particularly after Al tried to open a satellite version of it, "The Kite," on the UC campus. The investors got angry and accusatory; chaotic and hilarious things happened in the day-to-day operation of the place; personal dramas played out. But all in all, for the very brief time the Catalyst was in operation, the mood was vital, mellow and open. People who didn't know the original Catalyst think that the place Russell Kane bought is the same thing, but nothing could be further from the truth. Kane wanted a club, a hot music scene, and that's what he put in place. The ambiance was nearly the opposite of Al and Patti's Catalyst. Many people felt that the name itself should have dissolved with the place.

In any case, to this day I think it was one of the best jobs I've ever had. I worked with great people, all of them. I only mention first names here because. for various reasons, some people have chosen to put the 60s way behind them. Brock and Roger were the only two people who were on board at the Catalyst before I got there; we were all hired just as it opened. Later, when table service was added, Scott, Georgia, Cathy, Marilyn, and Karen became part of the crew. Sue, and later her husband, Dave, took back-up shifts at the counter once the business really began to roll. Diane, who had been at Manny's and the Sticky Wicket, and later opened Zachary's, made the chocolate crazy cakes in her home that we sold; Carli made the cheesecakes; this of course could never happen now, with food items and just about everything else so heavily regulated. All other food was purchased in the City, with Roger, stoned and naturally spacey anyway, trekking up there every few days in Al's funky truck that was prone to breaking down on the side of the road. There are so many stories with each of these characters, fun, funny, poignant, occasionally tragic. Many of the players are now gone, so this serves as a fond salute to them all.

724 CALIFORNIA STREET

While I was working at the Catalyst during lunch hours, Ralph Abraham came in. I had heard a little about him; the town was small and he was a relatively new guy, notorious for wearing a shirt made from an American flag, and as a result facing off with the uptight dean at UC. Never a fan of "the establishment" I felt an affinity with his viewpoint before I even met him. Apparently Ralph and his family were into macrobiotics, and he tried to convince me to get Al and Patti to agree to include brown rice as part of the deli offerings. This struck me as hilarious; the Catalyst food was basically NY Jewish delicatessen fare. I don't remember how that request turned out, but I was intrigued by Ralph. The head honcho at UC had labeled his household "musical beds," along with a few other pejoratives, yet when he came in with his wife and kids, he seemed reasonable enough. I had already spent some time in a couple of whacked-out communal-living situations, and his scene looked fairly grounded by comparison. We had some sparky flirtations over the counter, but it was all pretty innocent. That New Year's Eve my current boyfriend and I slathered our bodies with neon paint and danced onstage under black lights to a great amplified band. This was not new for me; while living in the Bay Area I had often danced onstage in various forms of dress, undress, or paint at the Avalon and Fillmore. The most important part of the 60s, to me, was — and still is — the music; I lived for it. This night was no exception: the band was fantastic, as was the whole evening. The place was packed with the big windowed doors flung open, letting reefer smoke waft in from curbside. Somehow that scene was a tipping point for Ralph and shortly after we ratcheted our flirtation up a notch. He would come to visit me at my beach house or we'd hang out in the beautiful secluded field, the vortex, at the University. I rarely went over to his house on California St. The big, rambling place was awesome; it reminded me of Jefferson Airplane's old Victorian in San Francisco. I couldn't get a handle on who was living there, other than the core group of Ralph, his wife Caroline, their two boys, and their beautiful golden retriever, Chester. People seemed to be constantly coming and going, mainly students I guessed. It was clear the place had taken a hit before he bought it, but little by little Ralph was attempting to make it habitable with repairs and fresh paint. Kids from the high school next door still congregated on the wrap-around front porch, but no one tried to break in and trash it as they had in the years when it sat empty. The kitchen was big and open, shaded by a huge walnut tree, and the kids rode their bikes right through whatever was going on there. The dining room was compact, with a formal feeling due to the built-ins that were always part of a place like that. A stereo system was placed against one wall, and next to it was Ralph's baby crib, filled with albums. There was always music playing, whether there was anyone in the room, or even in the house. Most of the bedrooms were on the second floor, and were reached from the wide embellished wood staircase at the front of the house. Unlike downstairs, these rooms were filled with light from ornately trimmed floor-to-ceiling windows. It was hard to tell whose bedroom was whose, other than the kids', and maybe that's part of what had caused the dean at UC to have such a burr up his butt. Up a steep, narrow staircase off the second floor was one of the crown jewels of the house — a cupola that looked out across the entire town. Many a soft morning was spent on the built-in bench seats up there at the top of the world, welcoming the rising sun after an MDA or acid-induced hallucinogenic night.

Not long ago, Ralph and I had the opportunity to go back into the house when it was put on the market for sale by the current owner. As generally seems to be the case, I remembered most of the downstairs rooms as larger than they are in reality. The walnut tree was gone, the cupola still unfinished. Our old room was fresh and clean; I had forgotten that it, like most of the upstairs rooms, also had an incredible view of the city. The kitchen was sleek and modern and basically unrecognizable. The house had been restored, and beautifully so, but the memories live on. Still, it was basically a different house ready for a new set of memories.

In early spring,1969, Ralph flew to England for a stint as a visiting professor at the University of Warwick. I flew over a month later, bringing his 6-year-old son with me. A couple of months later, Caroline followed, with their youngest son, and two of her friends. Our time in the UK deserves a book of its own; one someone else will have to write.

On our return, I moved into the Victorian with Ralph, since I had sublet my beach cottage to a friend for an indefinite amount of time. We came back to a house filled with students, over-run with fleas, and general chaos. Ralph and I took over a large corner bedroom on the second floor. I painted it pale yellow and put out the usual signs of the time: bed on the floor, madras bedspread and curtains, incense and candles, yarn gods' eyes, beaded necklaces on hooks on the wall. This was when things really ramped up at 724. The usual amount of people who came and went increased. Kesey would drop by with his whole group; they always conveniently showed up at dinner time. Joe Lysowski and his wife Wendy were living in an RV in the driveway; unlike Kesey, they left a light footprint. DW, a brilliant, unbalanced former math colleague of Ralph, would appear, disappear, then reappear. Ram Dass came and stayed in our yellow room upstairs; that was the only time people walked around in a somewhat hushed manner. Caroline went down to Esalen and brought back new people. And always, friends from before our trip to England came to visit, to eat, to take a pill.

On our return, Ralph had put white carpet in the living room, declared it a no-shoes space, and closed the door to the busyness of family activity. It was the de-facto sanctuary for group drugs, and many such sessions, mainly MDA, took place on that soft carpet. This was not a free-for-all drug have, at least during the time I was there, Ralph was predominantly a spiritual seeker. We somehow got a private audience with Chogyam Trungpa in Berkeley; sat front row at Krishnamurti's talk in Santa Cruz. Ram Dass didn't stay with us for the "wow" factor, but for the spiritual interest. And Ralph had sponsored his veena teacher from London, Shiv Batish and family, to come to America; while they looked for their own place to live, they stayed with us, and their presence had an immediate calming effect on 724. This was all a good counterpart to Kesey and some others who would blow through the house with a lot of noise.

As for me, I had no interest in being part of the entourage of the family. I had met Ralph, joined him in England, and would have been perfectly happy if no one else had shown up. Particularly infuriating for me was the prevailing patriarchal attitude at the time, with Kesey's group, and Kesey himself, being a good example, although they certainly weren't the only ones. They would come to the house, hang out and proceed to pontificate for hours. Women, myself included, were expected to feed them, humor them, and sleep with them. I couldn't believe how full of themselves they were — this was not necessarily intentional; they had never had cause to question their sense of entitlement. Now, so many years later, it's unlikely women would be content to stay barefoot and pregnant, keeping the hearth fire burning, baking the bread. Why didn't the women speak up? Some did, but the women's' movement was nascent at that time. Certainly all my female friends had opinions about this, and so did I. I also didn't have much desire to jump in and participate in the philosophical ramblings they took so seriously. I found their sense of self-involvement disgusting, and I began to fade from the scene.

ODYSSEY RECORDS

We were back from England, the Catalyst had been sold and was unrecognizable, Pacific Avenue had changed to Pacific Garden Mall, and I was hired as the manager for Odyssey Records. In some ways this was another dream job: music all the time, a free album with every paycheck, a great group of people to work with — Denis, Steve, Rick, Katie, Suzanne, Jimmy and especially Terry, my counterpart at the Monterey store. The owner of the store was into some shady stuff; we all heard rumors, none of us knew exactly what was true; none of us really wanted to know. Drugs were taking a hard turn; Jimmy OD'd on coke; a friend got part of her hand blown off when she was shot at trying to cross the border with pot. The mood on the street was very different from even a year before, nowhere near as light. While we were in England and trees were being planted up and down Pacific Garden Mall, Odyssey had moved from a tiny, dark space at the top of Pacific to a larger, brighter one next to the opposite side of the St. George from where the Catalyst had been. I'd ride my bike to work — the one Joe Lysowski had painted pink for me and covered with stickers. Someone stole that bike from in front of the store, but returned it the next day. Everyone was on the lookout for it, and only an imbecile would ride around on something that obvious. People tried to steal records, but given the size of an album it wasn't that easy to stuff a few in a sweatshirt. Steve or Denis would chase the culprit down the street; it was rare that anyone ever got away. Technically, as manager, it was my job to chase down a thief, but I made it clear I would never do that. So I got the worst end of the deal — I had to decide whether to call the cops or not. Lew Fein, best astrologer/best friend, had been in the previous small Odyssey, and he too moved to the new place. Every afternoon I made brown rice and veggies for the whole crew on a hot plate in a storage area in the back of the store. I had been into food in England and at 724, and continued it here. We were serious about macrobiotics, or so we thought. But macrobiotics is a balancing act, and there was no way that buckwheat could balance MDA, so eventually that fell by the wayside. To this day I have low tolerance for rice and veggies.

I had moved out of 724 and was staying with Al and Patti until my own house was vacated by the person I had rented it to. Over at California St. someone, Caroline I think, got interested in a yoga school down south. I went once with the whole family, and then by myself. I decided to move down there; later Ralph's family moved down as well, but it was the beginning of the end for them. Not long after, the family unraveled, resulting in an ugly divorce. Too many boyfriends, too many girlfriends, too many drugs, too many options. Jealousy, power plays, drama — probably the same as every other epoch on this planet. The 60s were over. It seemed like they had lasted a lifetime, but it had only been a few short years.

Part VI

The Barn, Summer 1966

9. Leon Tabory

I interviewed Leon on four occasions in 2002. The recordings were transcribed by Becky Leuning in 2003, and saved on the shelf. The later two transcriptions were recently combined and edited for this volume by Judy Lomba. Leon passed away September 29, 2009, at age 83.

Ralph: When you arrived in the U.S. after you were liberated from Dachau, where did you go?

Leon: I lived with my father and his new family in Baltimore. That didn't work out well: I barely knew him; plus I didn't agree with his orthodox religious beliefs. After a year I left Baltimore and moved to Brooklyn with my mother's relatives. I got a job as a laborer in a factory during the day and went to school at night. I went to the Rose Preparatory School, and then on to college. Then I moved to get away from that area altogether.

Ralph: And your first job?

Leon: My first job was as a counselor at the University of Wisconsin Counseling Center. I was a graduate student and I learned pretty quickly that I wasn't made for that institutionalized mould. They had training skills workshops that everyone had to fit into — the purpose was to try to get them back into the community. I didn't believe in it; I felt it was a very negative experience for some of the seriously retarded people there who were forced into participating. The administration was disappointed in me because vocation wasn't my religion, and so we parted company. Then I got a job at a Milwaukee Jewish vocational service where they had a new program that contracted with the United States Office of Rehabilitation. They, too, were focused on vocational skills, so again, a bad fit. I then took a job in a mental hospital, Furnace Falls State Hospital, in Minnesota. That was a very interesting, different scene. It was an old fashioned place — a huge productive farm that was maintained by the patients. It was run in an aristocratic way where we, the faculty and administration, all lived on the grounds, and the patients would prepare and serve us food in our own private dining room. We were referred to as "professors." The idea was to start bringing in new content and do treatment in ways that hadn't been tried before. I liked the idea but it was very cold in Minnesota, so I decided to go to coastal California, mostly because I had heard that you can go sailing all year long.

Ralph: You had become a devotee of sailing?

Leon: Extremely so. During my four years in graduate school in Madison I lived in the closest building to Lake Mendota. You could just run out there any time and grab a boat, sail around and come back to do some work whenever you wanted. And sailing was fun, so that's why I came to California. I applied to the civil service for a psychology job. I took the civil service exam, and lo and behold, I ended up ranking number two even though I didn't have a PhD. Civil service had a regulation that all available jobs had to be offered to the top three ranking candidates, so I started getting telegrams from all over. I ended up taking a job in San Quentin that was interesting for several reasons: First, it was right in the middle of the bay. Plus, I'd be staying in Tiburon, which was right across the water. But also the job itself was interesting. They had an intensive treatment program — a research project that was carried out in two places: Chino and San Quentin. There was a lot of money involved –. $300,000 a year for San Quentin alone. It was a very scientific program, with lots of staff and even more testing. They were studying recidivism; trying to be more effective in the way they handled inmates in an attempt to get away from just warehousing them. My job as psychologist was to suggest modifications to the program to make it more effective. I had studied with Carl Rogers, so they were interested in my ideas, and that was very exciting for me.

Ralph: So arriving in California — was this around 1960?

Leon: September-October 1957. I had this great house on stilts on the edge of Tiburon and I was working in San Quentin at a very interesting job. This was like a dream for me. When I first arrived in California, just to check out the job before deciding to take it, I drove into San Francisco one night. I didn't know the city at all. I drove to North Beach, which was one of the only places where things were happening at night. I had come here just to get a job at San Quentin, do some sailing, check out the area a little bit, and I land in the middle of North Beach in Beatnik land! I was wandering around and happened to go into Coffee Gallery. I started talking to the bartender there; I told him that I was new in town, and that I was a psychologist working at San Quentin. He said, "Oh! San Quentin! You've got to look up Neal Cassady. He's in there." I had read some of Kerouac's stuff so I knew a little about the beat scene, but the bartender piqued my curiosity. After I got settled in my office, I sent a docket for Neal to be brought in. I told him about meeting his friend, the bartender at Coffee Gallery, so that's how Neal and I met and became friends. Because of the design of the prison inmate program I was able to do my own research. I asked for a clerk from the prison population, and was sent a guy named Gene Fowler, who would later become a well known poet. He was a very gentle man, who came from a rough background and a hard tour in Korea — and well, his reaction to being in Korea is what landed him in Quentin. I ended up with four more clerks, so the group of six of us pretty much had a free hand to do what we wanted within this new intensive treatment plan. Among other things, we used Learys questionnaire. That was before we knew anything about his involvement with LSD.

Ralph: The Personality Assessment Questionnaire?

Leon: Yeah. The questionnaire was fascinating — it was just a list of 128 adjectives – and the things we were doing with it were really interesting. We learned a lot about the way the inmates thought. But the administration, which was very scientifically based and put a lot of value on testing, didn't see it the way we did. I had been brought in to offer innovative ideas, a lot of which they didn't like. Before long they were looking for ways to fire me. I was hoping to keep the data we had gathered using the questionnaire with the inmates so that I could work with it a little more. Nope, they said, that's our property. They confiscated that data and I never saw it again.

Ralph: So what happened?

Leon: Once a year every psychiatric social worker had to write a report to adult authorities about their clients, the people they'd seen for the past year. The inmates' parole depended on a clean report. Which meant the inmate was not likely to be fully honest during the course of the year if what he disclosed could jeopardize his chance at parole. So I called attention to the inherent fallacy of these reports and how they set the inmate up for gaming the system. This did not go over well with the authorities. The chief of research came from Sacramento to the warden's office to speak to me personally about my perspective as well as the fact that I had made it public through memos. It was obvious that politics were a big issue since he kept mentioning the governor and upcoming elections and funding for the program. Even though my only concern was doing good research that might benefit the inmates, he kept saying, "You don't understand corrections." Well, I was already a troublemaker in their eyes, so they terminated me. This was at the end of the year. But then immediately after that they got approval for funding for another year, so they rescinded and re-instated me. Not only that, but evidently they had considered what I said and decided to eliminate the year-end reports. I found this very encouraging so I decided it was good to speak up more about what I thought. But some people in administration still wanted me out of there and they started again to look for ways to make that happen. I then challenged a rule that said employees of the Department of Corrections are not allowed to associate with ex-convicts or their families. I said that it would be helpful to my clients if they could retain contact with me after they were on parole since we had already developed a client-therapist relationship. I wrote a memo to Sacramento to that effect, asking for permission to maintain relationships with ex-convicts, and surprise, that permission was granted, with the caveat that no personal matters could be discussed during meetings outside the prison setting. So that was good; they realized the benefit of the parolee being able to maintain contact with the therapist he had worked with for a year. In fact, they ended up stating that they were going to change the intensive treatment program to a "follow-through" program. But more troublesome for me, they told me it was now my job to design this new parole program. It had to be set up within the next four months, because funding happened at that time. I sent a memo that I had no idea how to set up a program like that because it had never been done before, and received a memo back that basically said, Figure it out; it's your idea and it's your job to make it happen. By that time I had been seeing Neal for about a year; he was ready to go out on parole. He had big family concerns and asked me to help out. That was right between the time they had given permission for me to see an inmate on parole as long as we didn't discuss anything personal, and the requirement that I create the follow-through program. Since they had told me to find out whatever was necessary to decide operational procedures for the new program I decided it was okay for me to get involved in Neal's family situation, particularly since Neal was ready to start the parole follow-through program as soon as it was in place. Neal let his parole officer know about our arrangement, and the guy freaked out: "What? A psychologist from San Quentin came to see you and your family? And you're talking about personal things? That's against the rules!" This complaint was sent to Sacramento where I was considered a troublemaker anyway, so they dumped the program and began the process of dumping me along with it. They transferred me to Vacaville, with the excuse that there was a shortage of psychological services there. So I was living in Tiburon but the San Quentin job was over, parole follow-through was over, and I was working in Vacaville. But I was there only a very short time because after the parole officer's report had gone through the channels and made its way to the top I got a telegram telling me I'd been fired. For willful disobedience and insubordination. Meanwhile I continued to see Neal and Carolyn because it no longer mattered since I wasn't working at San Quentin anyway. After all this, I went to the State Employees Association to ask for help, and also saw a few lawyers. I thought I had a reasonable case. They all said, "No. The Department of Corrections has a tough case against you. The rule is clear and you violated it." And so I decided to fight it myself. Ultimately I got it resolved, in a way. The hearing officer said that I had acted reasonably under the circumstances, which were unclear due to the time gap between my requested permission to see ex-convicts and the administration's order that I gather material for creating the follow-through program. But it didn't really make any difference. The research department claimed that we had philosophical differences and so they had the right to fire me. So even though it was considered a "moral victory" for me, I still had lost my job. And that was the end of it. But by that time, I had another job, a good one, at a mental health clinic in San Jose. It was near Neal's house so I moved in with them. They were living in Los Gatos. Neal had received $30,000 from his train accident and had bought a house.

Ralph: Train accident?

Leon: Yeah. When Neal had the accident on the train, they got $30,000 from the Federal Pacific or wherever he was a brakeman. I don't know exactly what happened. It derailed or something and he fell and got hurt. There was some medical settlement and he got $30,000.

Ralph: And what year was that?

Leon: When I came to Neal's house it was 1962. For two years I was without a job. I was just waiting to resolve the issue with San Quentin. I wasn't taking it lying down. And I was struggling. Part of what really got to me about the transfer to Vacaville was they lied to me. They said they were transferring me due to a lack of psychological help there. But in reality, they were punishing me. They even told me I wasn't allowed to take anything from my office — all my notes and files were state property. I guess they were hoping I would just quit. But I didn't quit because I was committed to fighting them. Instead, I called them on their lying. But all this took a while to work out, so I started to look for a new job because I wanted no more hassle. And that's when I got a job in San Jose in the mental health clinic and went to live at the Cassady's. In fact I lived with them until the hearing came up, and by then I already had a job.

Ralph: I'm interested in the sequence of events that got you from San Jose to Santa Cruz.

Leon: My move to Santa Cruz had nothing to do with beatniks or hip people or any of that at all. It was a professional thing. When I worked in the clinic in San Jose there was a clinical director, a psychiatrist, whose name was David McCarthy. David McCarthy and I became buddies. We would have dinner along with many other psychiatrists living in the area and we were all close friends. One of the psychiatrists from our clinic, Florence Tousent, became the first director of psychiatry when they opened up the El Camino Hospital, which was the first private psychiatric facility in the entire area. At that time the only place for mentally ill people was in Agnew State Hospital, which was a warehouse. Florence asked me to work with her and do therapy on the ward. And they paid me a good hourly wage. So for about a year I set up the therapy program at El Camino Hospital, and I worked with them.

Ralph: And you were working in the San Jose mental health clinic at the same time?

Leon: At first. After that I had my private practice in Los Gatos. Part of the week I was going there. I had a group therapy setup on the ward for the patients and their families too. I learned some very interesting things there. Lockheed was the first company at that time that managed to get a contract that gave them a hundred percent psychiatric coverage. It turned out that a lot of the patients who came to El Camino were from Lockheed. They carried a whole culture of elitism. Hey, these were the designers of the space programs and Moffett Field and all the other innovations and laboratories and whatever else was going on at the time, and they were the brightest and most successful and their income was mostly from government contracts, defense. But behind the scene some of the executives' wives were trying to commit suicide. They would be placed in Agnew if there wasn't some other kind of intervention. So Lockheed started a very high coverage program for psychiatric services and then people didn't have to go to Agnew any longer. Instead they were going to the most modern place with the best treatment, whatever they wanted. These were the people in my groups: the husbands and their wives and their young children. They were all dependent on the contracts they received. Most of the decision makers for those contracts were ex-generals or ex-high army people in Washington; these guys were the ones who were dispensing the grants. When they came out to California to inspect, the wives from Lockheed were expected to cater to them. So whether they're going to give a contract to the Lockheed guy or some competitor depended on how they're treated by this poor fucking asshole further down. That's what was really going on. And some wives couldn't handle it because of the stress since those contracts were the biggest success you could find in our society then, and they ended up in deep despair over the feeling that they had failed or would fail. So those were the people I worked with, and they liked me. So I feel I did a good job.

David McCarthy was involved in the next psychiatric facility that opened, and Florence, feeling I was a good man, talked to David and got me a job there. I didn't need to go through a job application or competition or anything. After that, a psychiatric facility opened up through the San Jose Hospital. There used to be a tuberculosis facility at Mount Hamilton where the observatories were but it was no longer active. So they transformed this facility into a psychiatric department at San Jose Hospital, and David McCarthy was hired to be in charge of that. He went from the clinic to there, and so naturally I was again invited to start a program there. After that, David McCarthy was asked to start a therapy program at the Santa Cruz General Hospital, where until that time they used to temporarily commit people until the court decided what to do with them — if they had to remain committed they were off to Agnew. But this time they decided they wanted to do something else there. And so who was invited to do the therapy, to start a therapy program there? I was already the man who was starting all the programs in the only private facilities that were opening up in the area. So that's how I got here. Plus David was always pushing me to come live in Santa Cruz. One of the times my sister Barbara came to visit me David invited us for dinner at the Shadowbrook to show us how beautiful Santa Cruz was. I remember that was one of the things that – ahh! – got me to Santa Cruz. And so that's what happened. I had my private practice in Los Gatos and I was coming to Santa Cruz a couple times a week.

Ralph: And did you maintain contact with Neal Cassady?

Leon: All throughout that time.

Ralph: And did you stay in contact with any other hip or beat characters or old friends from San Francisco?

Leon: I had a group of friends – let's see, Neal and his friends already were hanging around with them, they would sometimes drag them along to come to see me — there were a bunch of them. Followers kind of, young girls especially.

Ralph: So Ken Kesey and the Pranksters were hanging around?

Leon: No. There were a few times when Neal and I went to San Francisco or Marin – Kesey had moved to La Honda by then — and a couple of times I just stopped by with Neal.

Ralph: Jack Kerouac had already passed away?

Leon: No, he hadn't passed away yet but when Neal was in prison, Jack was really not nice. Actually, a lot of people had bad feelings about Neal: 'He always gets himself in trouble, you know, it's his own fault, don't help him out," that sort of thing. And in a certain way that would have been true if Neal had been asking for help but in fact he wasn't. So then it's just your own judgment, you know; he wasn't complaining about it. But a lot of people just couldn't deal with him.

Ralph: So you were doing your job in San Jose and Santa Cruz and maintained your friendship with Cassady.

Leon: I had a friendship; I never became too involved – I never dropped out from my life to move into their life at all.

Ralph: So there was no explicit interest in LSD, it was not happening yet around California...

Leon: Yes, yes, there was an interest. My interest in LSD actually was because of a speech by Leary — it was after he was through at Harvard, but before all the craziness, so to speak, and for the most part there was still a limited range of professionals looking at LSD and considering it as a professional tool. So I became very interested in that way. Also, when I was still at the San Jose clinic, there was a group in Palo Alto that had a foundation. They were giving LSD to patients under careful supervision and they were reporting some very great experiences. When I was a psychologist at the clinic and David McCarthy was still chief there I got my chance to go check them out and talk and it was very, very impressive stuff. So, yes, I was interested. But I was interested as a professional, wanting to get a better tool to work with. And I remember from the early days that Alpert — and Leary too — when they started they were more interested in it as a therapeutic tool.

Ralph: Before they applied the therapeutic tool to themselves too much and were transformed forever.

Leon: No, no, no, way before that. But there was so much pressure to make it available for others. And so they started a bunch of what I consider sort of rogue organizations to try to let that happen. Because there were so many people pressuring them for this, right? Would you want to deny anybody this? No. Would I? No. I still felt, though, there needed to be limits – I was never kindly disposed toward Kesey's group, the Pranksters. There was something about them I didn't like when they let their wild side out and I still feel this. So that's what notoriety and media and all these things do, but also what the drug did and I kind of felt it was really too bad. I think Leary or maybe Alpert were starting to put brakes on that as much as they could under the circumstances, trying to hold fast to their original ideas and philosophies and hopes — that was what was most important for them.

Ralph: I feel that we're right at the point of something here where you're okay, you have this professional interest in LSD, you're doing your professional work in Santa Cruz as well as San Jose. You're living in Los Gatos; you're going back and forth. Now I'd like to get from there to the Barn.

Leon: Okay, well you asked me how I got to Santa Cruz. It had nothing to do with LSD, even though LSD was going on in another part of my life. But it wasn't interfering with my life as a whole. In fact I did use LSD in my private practice too, very successfully. I never felt that you just used it to turn on and get high. I felt, and I still do, that it involved a lot of centering of oneself and appreciation, not just, "Let's go see a movie and see how great it is." You don't just, hey, get a drug and everything is going to work fine. You are a person before and you are a person after, and who you are and what you do with your opportunities is more important than the opportunity itself. It can work like this: you go through the opportunity and it transforms you. Anyway, I would have been fearful of the consequences if I just turned on at a party, thinking "Hey take some and see what it does for you."

Ralph: So how long were you commuting to Santa Cruz before you actually got involved in Santa Cruz and somehow found out about the Barn or got interested in getting that space?

Leon: Neal, who was coming around all the time, started talking to me about the Hip Pocket Bookstore. In fact, before it had opened, when they were still just planning it, he was telling me about the Pranksters and how Kesey and his friends were going to open up a bookstore and Peter Demma was the guy who was going to be the manager and that maybe I should give him a hand. He was going to give him a hand too and had started to do a little clerical work there. I would come around sometimes just to talk and see what was happening; see if I could help out. This didn't go on for long, maybe a matter of months after I had started to work in the hospital.

When I first started going to the Hip Pocket I used to hang out with one of the ladies from the Pranksters and her boyfriend. There was a cooler in the back of the store and we'd all go in there and smoke marijuana. So that was the thing, you know, I'd just go down to the Bookstore and we'd go into the cooler and smoke some grass. It was a good scene. And then the Christian Women for Morality formed at a Baptist church in Scotts Valley. They organized a telephone campaign; actually, it was a battle campaign, a war plan. There was a group of women who would call the Hip Pocket 85 times a day, saying "When are you going to take down the nude pictures?" This wasn't a question, it was a demand. The phone would ring again. "When are you going to take down the nude pictures?" And then again 15 minutes later

— constant insane, relentless harassment. As someone who was just filling in at the Bookstore, I go, "Fuck the pictures! Shit!" Honestly, that's the way it was. I thought, "I cannot deal with this." So I told Peter, "Not me. You need to get some other help." At the same time the poetry scene was just beginning. I knew this group of very active, militant poets in San Francisco. And I said, "Free speech! Let's start a free speech thing at the Hip Pocket Bookstore." I got them down to the Bookstore to make presentations. Meanwhile, we were being harassed by that Christian Women for Morality group, and I thought, Fuck, no need to make a war by telephone. So we said, "If you have something to say, come in and say it. Friday night's Free Speech night. Anybody who has any complaints or questions or wants to say something, come here and just say it." So that's how the free speech thing started in the Hip Pocket Bookstore. And it was very successful. Even without the Christian Women for Morality.

Then I heard that Eric Nord was opening up a coffee shop in Santa Cruz. What? Eric Nord? A coffee shop? I knew Eric Nord from San Francisco. When I first came to San Francisco and was hanging around North Beach, Eric Nord was the guy who had opened up the Hungry Eye with Enrico Banducci — it was one of the well known, popular comedy places and it did very, very well. But Eric Nord and a coffee shop – well I wasn't sure. In 1956, 1958, he started a thing in North Beach – a loft, a party loft. He said, "Hey you guys, you don't need to pay for entertainment just because you want to come out and hang together and drink a glass of wine. Come to my place. Use the place. Bring your own wine, bring your own entertainment, introduce yourself and just give a buck at the door and go in." That was a new thing then, and a good thing. Eric Nord was a starter. So that's when I met him. And I kept hearing things about him because he moved from there to Venice and wherever he went he started poetry groups, entertainment, music, whatever, and the place ended up becoming a cultural hub. But when I knew him, he had just started the poetry loft. He was an interesting person, you know. He had been in Hollywood a little bit, in real estate, and he was dropping out and living his life doing all these creative things and encouraging people to be part of it. And also, it turned out, encouraging in other ways. There were some very young girls, and he got busted for harboring runaways. I think that's what made him leave San Francisco. It was in the paper, so there went his reputation, and that's the last I heard of him.

So then I hear he's here in Santa Cruz, opening a bookstore! It turned out there was a woman who owned this place, the Barn, in Scotts Valley, and she had hired him to start a coffee shop there. I thought, great, I got to check that out, you know. So I went down there and I saw Eric Nord at the Barn and he tells me, "Oh yeah, I'm using this beautiful big place." There was this lady, this wonderful lady, she was just a manager at the telephone company but she wanted a business, she wanted to open up a coffee shop – exactly one of Eric's dreams, you know, and she hired him just to see if he could make it work. And paid him a salary. I said, "Wow, I've got to meet this woman. Who is this woman? That's the mother of my children."

10. Joe Lysowski

Joe told this story in a story circle meeting of the
Santa Cruz Hip History group, November 16, 2004.
The recording was transcribed by Becky Leuning,
posted to the website in October, 2015, and edited
recently for this volume by Judy Lomba.

Watching a movie on the 1960s I saw a film clip of Allen Ginsberg in a white robe dancing and chanting Hindu mantras. And
I thought, "I was there" at the place Bill Graham ran. I saw
some of my slides of Ron Boise's thunder machines being projected up on the theatre walls of the Family Dog. My mind
slips back, dimly reflecting the essence that illuminated those
times. How old I seem to myself, but the memories appear like
yesterday and even music from the Grateful Dead fills my ears.
What a great time it was; it felt free to be in San Francisco,
the great Love-in at the Golden Gate Park, riding to L.A. with
Neal Cassady driving the Kesey bus, a tube from the back porch
tank of nitrous oxide hanging from his mouth, being with Boise
going out to Texas to show our sculpture show to a bunch of
rednecks. We moved it over to Fort Worth. Happy, happy times
– all the communes – I saw them all. Drop with Libre, the Lama
Foundation. How strange, I thought, you pay people to let you
work on their property. That must be how religions get started.
Painting the Last Supper as a picnic table at Libre. Everyone
seemed to have a horse but I had the Boise van. Content to
exist on wheels on the road to nowhere. Yet being somewhere
– ever present in this past moment even as I speak of it now. I
was pure, full of love and gratitude for being alive. Camping,
eating brown rice in trailer parks in national campgrounds and
smelling the bacon and coffee others were cooking and knowing
and loving the difference; so happy that I was with my wife and
small son.

Early

But to really go back, to my earliest years, let me tell you about my family coming to California. I was only 7. They all only spoke English to me so I wouldn't have an accent. My grandmother belonged to a Russian Orthodox Church but we were all Catholic except for my father who didn't even sin and got out of going to church because of it. My grandfather came out and gave my dad a blackjack as we were ready to leave and for me he had a pipe wrench he made himself at the Mills. Grandma said there were black widow spiders in California and we'd be back soon. There weren't and we never were.

We came out to Santa Cruz where I saw the ocean for the first time by the Boardwalk. We all ran out into the sand together and loved it. My dad had all kinds of jobs at first. We'd pick fruit everywhere, my dad and I, apples in the mountains. I'd climb the long ladders and he'd hand the buckets down to me to dump in the box. He'd take on whatever work he could do, building stone walls or putting up fences and painting houses, and that continued until he met his friend who had a catering business and they cooked together. Then my dad got work at a small cafe at an old bar called Mac's Place in Boulder Creek. We'd drive up there early and he'd make a hundred chicken pot pies every weekend for a lot of bikers who would stop in to eat. After that he got into the Santa Cruz restaurants and I grew up there and in Scotts Valley where I'd go out and dig up sharks teeth to send to a guy who gave me ten cents each for them.

I did a lot of hiking around there near some old sand hills and a church camp. No one was around much so I'd drop trees down onto their trails to make the church-goers stronger for Jesus by having to climb over them. A lot of fun having a dog, an axe, and a BB gun as a kid.

I spent most of my time on the beach, surfing. I'd peddle down by bike from our house up by the city reservoir with my homemade boogie board of plywood – there were even more boards to throw and jump onto and slide before I got my Velzie Jacobs 9-foot 10inch Narrow Rail Long Board. Oh I loved that board – red bottom – hot dog! I'd run up and down the beach in prep for joining the Marine Corps the end of summer after high school, at 17. When I got a little older I drove a '37 Ford blue coupe convertible – white top, 88 flathead, Mercury engine, dual carbs, with a rumble seat in back open for my board. Loved that car too. Where did it all go? Time flickers faster, like pages in a well thumbed book as we look back on it. Like a cool breeze.

The Barn

Remember him? Cool Breeze, I mean, of the Pranksters. He was fun. He liked being a Neal Cassady protégé. He'd go movin' around the dance floor of the Barn where I worked doing light shows with Paul Curtis and Saul Mitig of Magic Theatre. "The price of admission is your mind" is what I remember. The Pranksters all stayed there after Ken had disappeared, leaving the bus parked with a note saying, "Ocean, Ocean, you have won" and his shoes left by the water's edge. My partner in sculpture, Ron Boise, drove him down to the border in a potato chip truck and rolled him up in a rug so he could avoid going to jail for smoking a joint with Mountain Girl. Ken had a fun house up in La Honda, 'Sky Londa,' where people used to inhale nitrous oxide, laughing gas, in the redwood grove outside the house. They talked real funny and would fall down having such a good time.

Funny, years later I'd end up working at the Barn for Lithuanian therapist Leon Tabory. He wanted the Barn to become a living theatre to enrich people's lives and strengthen their growth through dance, drama, music, and the arts. Leon was a man of the future whose parents were put into a concentration camp by the Nazis. How he escaped and made his way to America is a long story. Peter Demma of the Santa Cruz Hip Pocket Bookstore introduced us. Leon told me about his dream of expanding the Barn to show man's future – his evolution from the ocean to become what he is today — and to further help him up the ladder of consciousness. I tried to help him with this dream.

The entire downstairs of the Barn was done in an antique fashion, but upstairs what had been a gymnasium and basketball court became our theatre. To get the effect of a living ocean I painted the walls with a solid yellow background and over this a blue glaze, which I'd run along with my fingers pressed to the walls to make seaweed forms and images stand out with large-scale finger painting techniques. A dream of my own was reflected within one part, "Where are you silver love," of a goddess-like figure of shining silver. From the ceiling I hung large butterfly mannequins that Carl Speyer brought me for which I made wings of fiberglass; and outside a large iridescent sun symbol to match the giant shell symbol for gasoline that was on the local freeway. I cast it with the help of the boat-building Denson brothers of Maui over a mound of sand shaped upon a giant telephone pole. We packed the sand down and then laid strips of fiberglass over all of it. Then we lifted it up off the sand and I painted the front two ways: first to look like a normal sun with the light behind; then that light would go out and a black light would make it glow to symbolize our future direction.

The local church groups couldn't see it that way and called it the work of the devil. They raised petitions to shut down the Barn as a theatre and deny it use permits. They also claimed that trash such as beer cans and condoms had been left in the parking lot at night and somehow they felt that they were our used condoms and not those of their congregation. I went to a meeting and spoke in favor of Leon, who had been also speaking to women's clubs in Santa Cruz, advocating the use of marijuana and LSD in psychotherapy. Afterwards a newspaper wrote up a negative report on the Barn activities and my dad said, "You ought to get out of town, Joe. They're going to try and tar and feather your group with gossip and slander."

Life Drawing

Later, while I was teaching life drawing classes in my studio, I spoke to Vic Towers, owner of the Sticky Wicket, about my concern over this situation. He'd been coming to my drawing classes along with the president of the local Sierra Club. Vic said he'd been in the D.A.'s office and saw a list of people no longer needed in the community — my name was ninth on the list. So my time of teaching there was soon over. We did have a fun show of the drawings and paintings the Sierra Club president had created over the years. He was an old guy with knee-high boots laced up and drove a Land Rover. He built a clubhouse for himself to sing and perform a German opera and in between sets he'd show his artwork for everyone to vote upon — even the mayor of Santa Cruz was there and I was very proud. The class itself was unusual. I'd mix model couples together. My friend and fellow artist, soon to become "Minister Bob Casey," was a strong, good-looking guy and he loved to go up to the new University of California campus and choose a model to pose with that night. I'd put one of my spinning fiberglass wheels, designed by inventor artist Dr. Richard Smith, into action behind them – looking like a Persian rug powered by a variable speed motor and variable speed strobe light — turn up the music, serve wine and we'd draw and paint for hours, all for $2 a person. What fun! Art and motion, alive.

Artist Al Johnsen had quit hanging paper walls for a living and turned to doing pottery at his Scotts Creek Pottery. He had a strong vocal belief in mankind's work. Hoye Parton and Manny Santana opened up Manny's restaurant in Aptos and we'd go there for late dinners. Manny became a colorful artist with his son, Luis, and was loved by all. These were my friends in powerful times, changing times, "for the winds they are a changing" Bob Dylan kind-of-times. Futzy Nutzle, a.k.a. Bruce Kleinsmith, started a newspaper with Spinney Walker and Henry Humble to parody these times and the flavor of Santa Cruz ... caught in the winds of change, some say it was like a vortex of energy. Ralph Abraham, mathematician at UCSC, brought many leaders to speak on campus, like Richard Alpert, soon to be Baba Ram Dass, who was spending much of his time in India.

India

I also had the urge to go to the home of Gandhi and Krishnamurti. While reading the Upanishads, the Bhagavad Gita became my religious inspirational source and soon I found myself heading to the Hindu holy lands with the lady who became my wife of 22 years, Wendy. I felt the powerful draw of Hindu philosophy and science. I wanted to explore this land of the Book of the Dead and the Bardo Thodal. We landed in Delhi and caught a bus up to Rishikesh, 16 hours away, entranced by this large and different country.

Of course, we weren't the only ones to head to India during this time. The Beatles followed their guru, Maharishi Mahesh Yogi, and many people followed them. We were introduced to Maharishi, who gave us jobs to do in return for our mantras — Hindu holy words of vibration, and I had the strong feeling that these vibrato were going to change the world through meditation. We met many rock stars during our time there, including the Beatles, but I didn't pay much attention to any of them, thinking that we were all on the same level of being, and that the only thing that separated them from us was money.

At one point George Harrison and Paul McCartney were telling me about the far-out movie they had made called "Help" and asked what I'd been doing. I told them of the thunder machines made by my partner, Ron Boise. I explained that they were large musical instruments designed to help musicians develop new ways of creating musical sound, a way to break traditional habits; and then went on to talk about what it was like in America, in California in the '60s, the political scene going on there and my wanting peace so bad for Viet Nam. What would it take for peace on Earth? Could we make any changes? I hoped our just being there in India would help a country where I felt the foundation of religion had started.

Texas

I'd worked on painting the large thunder machines for a show at Anchor Steam Beer in San Francisco. That was before taking them on to Dallas "fucking" Texas. The show was on the roof and we made the Chronicle with a picture and an interview with a reporter. Then we left on the tedious drive to Texas in a potato chip van and long old flatbed truck which was lashed down with psychedelic painted sculpture I'd worked on with Ron. We were stopped 23 times on that drive. The police just couldn't believe us. They'd pass, their jaws would drop, and they'd wheel around on the highways to stop and talk to us. Another time we went down to Foster City in Ray's old VW which was primed matte black, all our art packed into it to do a light show for the Art League there. We had many adventures that involved new art and old cars.

Coda

Wind me back, wind me back like some clock to an earlier time, to us 41 happy hippies in a commune with nature. Not as far back as the Marine Corps at 17. I was too young for that. I wasn't ready to kill; nor was I ready for the deaths of those who have passed from this life. The Ron Boises, Neal Cassadys, Jerry Garcias — all from a time past, dim as I review being there. We were younger and face to face with reality and our part in changing it. Wind me past the times picking fruit in the valleys of California with Father. Somewhere between the hospitals of the military and times I almost died in New Delhi, feverish from hepatitis and the doc there saying I'd be lucky to leave alive. Take me to the happy times: a first marriage, thinking this was it, church and all. Grand Baroque silverware place settings, we were there in heaven's hands. Past lobsters I wouldn't kill but returned to the ocean, past spiders I'd let go — perhaps I was a predetermined Buddhist. Given some hard shakes to help stir up compassion in me, gratitude for life. I love it — being here — every day breathing, just breathing, what others take for granted. Fun is a paycheck that always seemed to roll. Oh Goddess within my heart, compassionate one, loving-kindness one, love who sees me as I am and it's okay, who sees me as I'm not and it's okay. This isn't a rehearsal. This world full of tragedies and happiness is short lived. Don't desire too much.

Part VII

Pacific High School, Fall 1966

11. Fred McPherson

Written by Fred, December 2010.

Coming to Pacific High School in the Santa Cruz Mountains

Who knows whether the circumstances and network of cause and effect that brought me to the Santa Cruz Mountains and Pacific High School were a matter of chance or destiny? Coming to this area involved both leaving something that I had had enough of and a search for something new and better. I had a deep longing and conviction that there had to be a better way of life, a more spiritual path to fulfillment, and Pacific High School was the choice that I made to look for those things.

Reflections on the Times

My thoughts about the Pacific High School experience come within a social, political, and spiritual perspective of transformation. Not only did I make a change in how I taught science and how I understood knowledge and teaching, but I did it within the context of a radical process of transformation of death and rebirth which involved withdrawing from an economic and social structure that supported nuclear insanity and the constant threat of nuclear annihilation, the draft, the Vietnam War, and strange new drug and health laws that promoted reefer madness mentality, use of cigarettes, alcohol, pesticides, waste of our natural resources, and ongoing environmental degradation.

Deciding to Come to Pacific High School

I came to teach at Pacific High School from a very well-paying (for a teacher) position teaching science with the Bakersfield School District. At the time it was one of the most affluent school districts in California because of property taxes and oil revenues in the area. I taught Biology and other science classes at Burrows High School, out at the Naval Ordinance Test Center at China Lake in the Mojave Desert. It was the far-flung part of the Bakersfield School District. I was recruited for this position while working on my Master's Degree at the University of Chicago.

When I graduated in 1964, there was competition to hire young, newly trained science teachers with a background in biochemistry, molecular biology and training in the newest Biological Science Curriculum Studies (BSCS) science program. I was brought to Burrows High to launch the new BSCS Biology program and implement the new reforms in science education ushered in by the launch of Sputnik in the late 1950's. In addition to the Navy's regular personnel, there were a lot of technical science people on the base who wanted the best possible science education for their children. Not everyone recruited to teach at China Lake was interested in teaching there once they found out it was a dry lake out in the middle of the Mojave Desert at a Naval Ordinance Test Center, so, as a bonus for coming on board, teachers were given very cheap housing on the China Lake Naval Base along with other perks like base shopping, Officer's Club privileges, and other discounts.

Eleanor, my wife at the time, had a good job working for the Behavioral Science Division on the base. We had two well-maintained vehicles, good benefits, and a great dog, Quimick. Living on the base and in the desert was adventurous and also very beautiful in its own way. It could be very hot there in the summer, but the desert has an alluring beauty, smell, and feel that is very majestic. Despite all of these advantages, we lived on base at the Navy's Ordinance Test Center which was dedicated to researching and testing ways to make better bombs, napalm and weapons for use in the Vietnam "war" and elsewhere. Seeing magazine photos and TV news clips of Vietnam villagers running from their homes on fire used to bring me profound sadness and regret for my involvement in even teaching science at this military installation.

When offered the opportunity to do Ethology (Animal Behavior) research on newly captured bottle-nosed porpoises as they were brought into conditions of captivity for the Navy's porpoise project facility at Point Magu, California, I became very excited. But as I got further into my research, I became aware that the program was harmful to the porpoises and that the research that I was involved with had the potential of using porpoises to sink ships.

Even though I dearly enjoyed the beauty of the desert as well as teaching Biology, these concerns of conscience grew on me. It seemed increasingly necessary to find new ways of learning, being, and earning a living. The art teacher at Burrows High School, Mrs. Haig, told me about an experimental high school in the San Francisco Bay Area called Pacific High School. It was dedicated to an experience-based form of education. We investigated, and eventually decided to take part in the experiment. The search for a new spirituality and right livelihood seemed like the right path, and I am glad that we made the choice to be involved.

On the other hand, there were many sacrifices and mistakes that were made in this transformational process on a personal and collective level. Unexpected and unintended things happen, for better or worse, when you open yourself up for new experiences and growth. Most of the staff made major financial sacrifices to teach at Pacific High and "make it work." I remember that I felt so strongly about not supporting the war and "the system" that I took all of my money out of our savings and my State Teachers Retirement System (STRS) account to live on and headed for Pacific.

As we headed for our new life at Pacific High we had two well-maintained vehicles, a nice old single lens camera, our household possessions, and a dog. I was quite happy to take a big cut in pay to come to teach at Pacific at first, but as my salary shrank, and eventually got turned into two salaries for two full-time people without travel allowances or vehicle maintenance funds, I eventually ended up selling our vehicles because I couldn't afford to keep them up. Luckily, we did not have any health or dental needs while at Pacific, but the lack of health benefits (or any retirement benefits) and the devastating effect of a continual downward level of income contributed to involuntary simplicity and lifestyle changes that may not have been for the best. It was also a time of letting go of old relationships and for making new ones, and this is always a hard thing to do.

Early Days at Pacific 1966-67

When I first started teaching Biology and Science at Pacific we were still building the "Science Room." We had a few odds and ends of science equipment and a few old text books — not much to teach BSCS Biology and Science as Inquiry in the way that I had in public high school. I tried doing various experiments and labs that I could adapt from my past science backgrounds, but soon found that this was not of much interest to most of the students there. This was due not only to the lack of facilities, and my lack of experience, but also to a reaction against that old science classroom/traditional high school lab approach to education in general.

As I got to know the students and staff better, a new kind of curriculum began to develop. Out of the traditional Sex, Drugs, and Rock-and-Roll teenage curriculum, individual students and various-sized groups of students formed to learn more not only about the pharmacology and physiology of drugs and diet but the natural history of the surrounding Santa Cruz Mountains. I went with various groups of students into the back country to explore edibles and the environs around the cabins behind the school, and "Devils Canyon" to the North, where the run-away "hippie" children and diggers lived. One time a group of us went cross-country through logging sites to Memorial County Park and Pescadero Creek. The students and I ended up attending logging permit hearings and getting involved in the preservation of redwoods, even to the point of following loaded logging trucks to their destination at the docks where the logs were shipped to Japan. There was a lot of interest in useful and healing native plants, herbology, organic gardening, and logging and other con-servation issues as well as constant interest in the Vietnam War protests, the Draft, and Music and Dancing of the times in San

Francisco and at the Barn in Scotts Valley. More than once did
we load up the old school bus and go dancing on a Friday night
up at the Avalon or Fillmore ballrooms.

Early Days Staff 1966-67

When we first traveled to Pacific to meet the staff and students
for interviews, we interacted mostly with people like Alan Stran
and Stan Bean and briefly with a few of the students. When
we moved to the Bay Area we found housing for us and our dog
in Redwood Estates. It was the closest affordable place that we
could find where we could also keep our dog at the time. When
we officially started teaching there in the fall of 1966, we met the
rest of the full-and part-time staff. In addition to Eleanor and
I, who were considered the Anthropology and Biology teachers,
the other full-time teachers were Warren Howe, English Teacher;
George Hall, Building Construction Coordinator and Teacher;
Ken Kinzie and his wife Patty (who later changed her name to
Raven), Art Teachers; John Dufford (Sulumon), Music Teacher;
and Ray Ditman (and his Wife Bonnie), Math Teacher and Bus
Driver. Gloria Harmon (from Bridge Mountain in Ben Lomond)
was a part-time teacher in sensitivity training who attended staff
meetings and the early staff marathons and had a daughter,
Holly, who attended Pacific. Erick Trojack was one of the bus
drivers and had a sister, Nina, who was a student at Pacific.
Alan Stran and many others volunteered help with the on-going
construction projects. Stan Bean was our executive director and
Bonnie Ditman (Ray's wife) worked with Stan in the office.

We had regular staff meetings, board meetings, and several weekend-long staff retreats facilitated by Samtio Chung.
They were rather unique in that they were 48-hour marathons
(where participants stay awake for 48 hours) that employed a lot
of interesting improvisational "psycho-drama" and "encounter
group" techniques. Even though there were some pros and cons
to this type of intensive interaction, it seemed to help us learn
about each other in an in-depth way and encourage each other
as teachers and individuals.

Later in 1967 and 1968 other part-time teachers and facilitators for special classes and school-wide programs were added to the program. Alan and Heath (from Ananda) taught yoga several times a week. Aaron Manganelo was our Social Studies-community activist teacher. Jack Spicer also taught English. Jade taught about Viet Nam culture. Mike Murphy and others brought interns from Esalen to do body awareness-dance workshops with our students. Samtio Chung did improvisational drama with the students. This activity eventually turned into a full-fledged teenage anti-war guerrilla theater group that went onto various high school campuses to do lunch-time performances and workshops for administrators. Lars Speer was hired to teach Photography for awhile. He helped students and staff put together the first published Pacific newsletter. I am sure there are others that I am not remembering to mention. We discussed hiring these people at our staff meetings, but I was too much involved with teaching to be involved with the official contracts, staff budget, and paperwork for them. I was on the Pacific Board of Directors as a teacher representative for awhile. I was grateful to spend most of my time interacting and teaching the students and trying to keep my ever-changing life together rather than getting involved with a lot of administrative tasks.

All in all it was a dynamic, diverse learning environment for all concerned. I have made digital copies of my 35 mm slide photos of staff, students, field trips and life at Pacific High for Holly Harmon to use in her book about that era at Pacific High and the Holiday Cabins and Bridge Mountain in Ben Lomond.

Drop-in Teachers

There were still other people who acted as "drop-in" teachers. For example, there were wood-cutters like Austin Keith and Dave Sivilla and others who lived in the back country cabins behind the school who would stop by to visit as they drove through. There was Jafu Feng who would now and then walk to the school from his "Still Point" retreat on upper Bear Creek Road and do tai chi with us and discuss life. He was a great inspiration to me and was also one of the first tai chi teachers at Esalen. It was always interesting to have a celebrity like Wavy Gravy or other Pranksters drop in for a visit. Many parents would stop by for visits or to share something of interest with students. One day on my way up to Pacific from Palo Alto, I witnessed a pack of dogs running down a young deer along upper Page Mill Road. They had just brought it down. I stopped to see the deer and found its spirit departed, so I brought it to the school for our Biology lesson of the day. We learned a lot about mammalian anatomy and much more as we dressed the deer, skinned it and roasted it for an afternoon feast. Jafu just happened to stop by and share in the offering of the deer's meat for our feast. It was a moving Biology lesson for all and we considered the deer also to be one of our honored drop-in teachers.

Spiritual Adventure and Awakening

We did all of this largely on faith that we could create a better form of education and way of life in general. In the absence of any one spiritual philosophy, group of elders, guidelines, or culture to support community health and healthy relationships, Pacific High was sort of like a psychedelic amalgamation of many spiritual points of view and practices. There was a lot of input from the original Palo Alto Quaker community, who had a lot to do with the founding of Pacific High School as it grew out of Peninsula Elementary School. In addition to Jafu Feng's tai chi, and Samtio Chung's Subud, there were many other religious, mystic, and pagan insights and practices that were shared which influenced us all. We were largely in unexplored territory. It was a great blessing and opportunity for spiritual discovery, growth, and transformation on one hand, but such change can be difficult and it took a heavy toll on some.

My fondest memories of Pacific were the great field trip expeditions and the all-school experiments and adventures in experiential education that we pulled off. We had many great in-depth field trips and study groups that included political protests about the Vietnam War and logging of redwoods in the Santa Cruz Mountains; trips in the school bus to hear great music in San Francisco; musical and dance events at the school, like jam sessions with Max Hartstein and the 25th Century Ensemble, Bridge Mountain, and Esalen-led sensitivity training sessions; and nature hikes in the back country as mentioned previously. Science field trips to the Coastal Mountains, Great Valley, Sierra, and deserts to the east to study the Geology of California (as understood before the plate tectonic revolution); field trips to Hopi land and Mexico; newsletters and art projects; as well as the all-school events where we temporarily turned Pacific into such things as a Black Panther training center (without guns) and a Zen monastery with Shunryu Suzuki Roshi were some of the highlights for me.

As I scan slides for a Pacific reunion for 2010 and possible use for Holly Harmon's book, many old memories, images, and emotions come up. I am also impressed that from my current perspective as a retired public and private school Biology teacher (after about 40 years) and lecturer in Natural History at UCSC, as well as a husband, father to a beautiful daughter and wonderful son-in-law, and grandfather of two fine (Charter 25 home school) grandchildren who live in Zayante, how wonderful it was for the students and staff of Pacific to have those great experiences.

Despite our ignorance and the mistakes that may have been made, there was a great energy and sense of adventure and idealism at Pacific. Those kinds of quality, in-depth, experiential, small-group learning opportunities are not that common. Also, in retrospect, I think that despite my personal ignorance about the pitfalls of this type of educational experimentation, Pacific High and those students were fortunate to have someone like myself, who did have a really good academic Biology education background as well as a sense of adventure and willingness to let go of old ways of teaching and explore new areas of learning based upon student interests. Beside that, they were fortunate to get two teachers for the price of one low salary; and we did have that fine International Harvester (IH) Travel-All that ran well and took them on many great distant and local field-trip adventures.

Field Trip Notes

For example, in the California Geology class (field experience) and the Macrobiotic Diet Desert Seminar, they actually had a chance to travel together in the old IH Travel-All out across the San Joaquin Valley, over the snow-covered Sierra, across the Mojave Desert to Death Valley and back. Another time, a group of students wanted to live on a macrobiotic diet (one of the interests at the time) in an isolated area. We decided to have a Desert Seminar and travel to the Eureka Dunes, which were located in Saline Valley (just this side of Death Valley) and live on a brown rice macrobiotic diet for 2 weeks while studying the natural history of the desert. To have those kinds of first-hand experiences, as well as others along our coast in the ocean class to the Big Sur Coast to the South, into the north during the Marin County adventure, was a profound experience for me and hopefully for those students as well. Those teaching experiences changed my concept of education and life.

The Reunions

Perhaps the reunions that we have will in some way help us to experience coming out the other side of those chaotic times and there will be some perspective, resolution, healing, and appreciation of each other and our times together. I know that I really enjoyed meeting old students and staff again at the last reunion that I attended. I witnessed how our time together at Pacific was just one point in our lives and that we have all gone on to other things. It was a great time to give thanks, celebrate our accomplishments, meet the children, honor those who are no longer with us, go through my slides and try to make sense of and honor that time in my life.

Part VIII

724 California Street, Fall 1968

12. Ralph Abraham

Our community at 724 California Street, Santa Cruz, from September 1968 through June 1970, included my nuclear family (my wife Caroline, our two boys, Peter and John, and our dog Chester) and a shifting number of others, most notably Karen Akins (now Rivkah Barmore), Judy Hill, and Shanta and S.D. Batish. Due to my twin commitments to the hip culture downtown and the UCSC drama up on the hill, the 724 house became the meeting place for several groups.

This story was recorded in an interview with David Thiermann, January 14, 1989, and transcribed and posted to our Hip History website January 16, 2003. I recently updated it for this volume.

First visit to Santa Cruz, March, 1968

From 1964 to 1968 I was an assistant professor of mathematics at Princeton University, married to Caroline, with two small children. Suddenly, in March 1968, I received an invitation to join the faculty at UCSC as an associate professor with tenure. This was the occasion for a visit to Santa Cruz and my decision to move there.

I had been in Vermont for family and skiing. Page Stegner was there working as a ski instructor. We had been friends for a couple of years. He had told me about some colleagues or former fellow students in Santa Cruz, Jim Houston and Fred Shanahan.

When I got to Santa Cruz I tried to track these people down. I went to Jim Houston's house. He said that if I really wanted to find Fred Shanahan, I would have to go to the Barn. He gave me directions. I rented a car and drove out to the Barn. It was the place that Leon Tabory was running as a sort of psychedelic social experiment, you might say. I went there looking for Fred Shanahan and got my mind blown. There were paintings all over the walls by Joe Lyzowski, whom I later got to know –

fluorescent paintings with black lights shining on them. A band
from Big Sur was playing. These people (it was said) actually
lived in trees there. They had some kind of musical instruments
that nobody had ever seen before – sculptures by Ron Boise.
Tree people from Big Sur playing sculptures by Ron Boise under black lights for an audience of three hundred people–men,
women and children–all of whom (it seemed to me) were stoned
on acid. My mind was blown.

I met Cheryl, Peter Demma's sister-in-law. Through her I
met Peter. He was the co-founder of the Hip Pocket Bookstore
along with Ron Bevirt, one of the original hippies of downtown
Santa Cruz. I decided to accept the offer from U.C. Santa Cruz.
Although I wasn't very impressed by the University, I really
liked the town. As a neophyte acid-head myself I could see
the possibilities for enormous emotional, physical, moral, and
material support for the explorations that I was involved in,
including the politics and everything.

First Academic Year, 1968-69

The summer of 1968 was crucial for the movements of 1960s:
civil rights, anti-war, students' role in university affairs, and so
on. Also for mathematics, and my family relocation to California. There was an important math conference in Berkeley,
which I attended with a group of my students and colleagues
from Princeton.After the conference I drove to Santa Cruz to
look for a house.

Page Stegner, already ensconced at UCSC, told me of an
unusual opportunity: a derelict Victorian mansion at 724 California Street, next to Santa Cruz High school. It was among
the oldest homes in the county. Having been foreclosed, it was
for sale by a bank. It was a mess, damaged by fire, infested
with fleas, and a steal for $16,000. I bought it and we moved
in: Caroline, Peter, John, and two friends, Mandy and Karen.
We cleaned it up, furnished it, unpacked our things from Princeton, and rented the extra rooms to students and hippies. Soon
we were a community, home to many meetings and group trips

using LSD, MDA, and other substances. The community expanded with the addition of a few live-in vans in the yard. One was the bread truck previously owned by Ron Boise, among the first hippie mobile homes in California. It had been inherited by Joe Lyzowski after Boise's death, and was occupied by Joe, his wife Wendy, and small baby.

Our diet drifted toward the vegetarian, natural, organic, local, and bulk. Karen Akins led our bread baking with freshly ground organic whole wheat, and sold our extra loaves at the Catalyst Coffee House and Delicatessen, where she worked.

Local special interest groups held weekly meetings at 724: Gurdjieff readings, the I Ching, astrology. Sufi meditation, free schooling, and macrobiotic cooking among them. Macrobiotic dinner parties were organized for passing dignitaries such as Kirby Hensley, founder of the Universal Life Church, or Baba Ram Dass, who lived with us for a few weeks. Ken Kesey and the Merry Pranksters stopped by to visit. Local leaders like Al Diludovico, Lew Fein, Max Hartstein, the Lingemann community, and Peter Demma were regulars.

Early in my first year at UCSC I got into trouble for leading a student parade protesting the UC Regents, including Ronald Reagan. It was there I met Professor Paul Lee, who marched with me. My conflict with the UCSC administration escalated over a proposal for UCSC presented by Bill Moore, associated with the Black Panther Party, who became a regular visitor of our 724 community.

Part of my employment package at UCSC was an early sabbatical quarter, so in March I left for London and Coventry. Soon the extended family followed (now including Judy Hill) and we settled in an apartment on Molyneux Street in London, where all our hip habits continued and led us into all manner of adventures with the nascent hip communities evolving there.

In one of the first macrobiotic restaurants in London, I picked up a copy of a small magazine, *MusicAsia*, devoted to Indian music. Inspired by Hazrat Inayat Khan, Sufi musician and founder of the Sufi Order International, I had been looking for a way to learn to play the Veena. And here it was! S.D. Batish, noted

Indian musician and creator of *MusicAsia*, was offering lessons in Indian music in London. I became his devoted student during my six months in London, and eventually arranged a position for him to teach Indian music at UCSC.

Second Academic Year, 1969-70

In September of 1969 I returned to 724 California Street with the whole family. Both the hip habits and the conflict with the UCSC administration resumed. But this time, the presence of S.D. Batish and his wife Shanta transformed and elevated our home culture with saintly spiritual music and food.

During this period, through Ralph Metzner, we became involved with Russell Schofield, leader of the Agni Yoga cult (aka the School of Activism), and many of us moved to Valley Center, California, for the summer of 1970, to study with him. This move split our family, and ended the experiment of 724 California Street.

13. Rivkah Barmore

Rivkah wrote this story recently for this volume.

Memories of a Victorian

The majestic Victorian was on California Street in Santa Cruz California. During the late 60s — early 70s, the Victorian was owned by Professor Ralph Abraham and his wife Caroline. When I came to live inside this magnificent structure I was twenty-one or so. I believed myself most fortunate to have been invited to be a "helper," for Caroline; caring for the Abraham boys, Peter and Johnny.

The Victorian home was captivating. The light which shown through the large-paneled windows was bright, clean with occasional rainbows shining on the wall from the beveling. The air was always a bit chilled; I assumed due to the three stories, including a cupola, which made heating the Victorian a challenge. In the yard of the Victorian was a large walnut tree with a swing for the boys and shade for the family dog, Chester.

I met Caroline first through our mutual friend Ernie. Ernie also lived in a Victorian home on the corner of 7th and Soquel Avenues. All of us called Ernie's Victorian "The Trip House." Pretty self evident that Ernie's Victorian was the place to be on your LSD trip. I think Caroline, a professional photographer, found Ernie's Victorian (as well as Ernie) fascinating and an opportunity for a great photographic history of the era. I still have the photo of our "Tribe" which Caroline took. All of us: Ernie, Juan, (my love of many years), Rodney (a friend), Artie (Juan's cousin), Brian (Juan's brother), me, Lucy (a friend), and Artie's girlfriend, Trina. We were in our finest leather, lace, feathers, beads and long hair. Beautiful.

Back to the Victorian. I came in at Caroline's request. I helped her with the boys, I cooked macrobiotic meals for everyone, and I suppose I cleaned a little bit too. I had a little room on the second level of the home, close to the boys' rooms. I loved hanging out with the boys and Chester. I loved making organic, stone-ground bread which doubled as a brick after eighteen hours. We all ate a lot of brown rice, carrots and fertilized eggs. I also worked at the Catalyst as a server, and the Bookshop Santa Cruz. When the Catalyst was open from Front Street, the customers could walk through to the Bookshop. The owners at the time were Ron and Sharon, also friends within the "Tribe."

I am unsure exactly when I first met Ralph. The Victorian was so big I think I had been in the house for awhile before we met. When we did see one another inside the Victorian I realized he had been a customer at the Catalyst. I was very impressed with his intelligence and his sense of awe when he was with his children. In my little room the light streamed in through a western window. There were bright colors on the covers and pillows. I loved this small room. I would retreat to this room for meditation and naps. On one such occasion I experienced my first "out of body" perception. Amazing memory. Vivid and very real.

Caroline and Ralph had an open marriage. I also don't remember when Ralph and I became lovers. I do, however, remember lying awake for hours after our lovemaking, listening to Ralph illuminate mathematical themes, concepts, hopes for future projects and fantastic, futuristic musings; mostly being snug in a single bed, in a small room, in the Victorian.

A very clear memory within the Victorian was the visit from D.W. I was asked to oversee his visit while the family was on an excursion. He stayed downstairs. He rarely came out of his room. When he did appear he had his head covered and dark glasses on with only a small hole to look out of. He wouldn't say a word to me. However, once in his room, and going through whatever changes he was, he would howl, scream, bang on the walls. This pattern repeated for over a week, then he left the Victorian as mysteriously as he had come — without a word.

I lived at the Victorian without Juan. One morning I woke up with Juan sitting on the stairs to the second story. He had been up all night on an LSD trip. Apparently he'd let himself in and was waiting for me to wake up. Ralph had already left for class and so they had not seen one another. He was still in an altered state. He wanted me to move back to the ranch with him; previously Ken Kesey's ranch.

I asked for time to think about what I wanted. I was pretty happy at the Victorian. I decided to stay at the Victorian; after all there was a constant flood of visiting mystics, musicians, magicians, mathematicians and mad-men. Sometimes these wondrous individual qualities were found in one person; why would I leave?

The Catalyst, my part-time job, hosted an active venue for many artists. There was open mic night; poetry night, belly dancers often provided lively entertainment. When nothing formal was going on there were always intense conversations over coffee. Gurdjieff, Herman Hesse, who has the best LSD, all with Erik Satie on the sound system.

There was a "walk-through" to the old Bookshop Santa Cruz. One passed a turn-of-the-century fountain. Reflecting on this ivy-covered flow-through from the Catalyst to the Bookshop: it was the symbol of the flow of information, ideas. energy, light. It was beautiful.

Carlos Castaneda gave a book-signing and lecture around his book "Travels With Don Juan." After walking from the Bookshop, through the Fountain Room to the Catalyst he was heard to remark, "This is like walking through the Soul of the city."

I audited many classes at the university. The university system allowed students to audit as long as the professor agreed. During the spring of 1968-69, or so, the Freudian psychologist, Dr. Norman O. Brown, was a visiting professor at UCSC. His book, "Life Against Death," was a psychoanalytical history of war, a struggle between Eros and Thanatos. His lectures were always well attended and sparked much debate at the Catalyst/Bookshop later on. Dr. Brown was often included in these post-lecture discussions as well as at student parties; he was very popular and accessible. The last day of his classes the lecture hall was disrupted with individuals dressed as eight-foot penises, huge hairy balls, with all performers throwing tennis balls into the audience. It was a hit; perfect ending to the quarter.

Ralph was invited to lecture for the summer in Coventry. The whole family prepared to leave for England. Ernie was also invited to go with the family as well as others whose names escape me at this point.

Shortly before we were to leave for England, Caroline called me to the dining room. Caroline, (even though she had invited me to live in the Victorian with the family), reported to me that she had been living a nightmare. I was the cause of her nightmare and she wanted me out of the house. I was speechless. I left the meeting and went to my room. I couldn't figure out what I had done. We, Ralph, Caroline and I, were all in agreement with the sleeping arrangements, so I was clueless; young and clueless.

As it turned out, I stayed at the Victorian while Ralph, family and friends left for England. I was gone from the Victorian when the family returned. I loved living in the Victorian and love those who so profoundly influenced my life. Good memories of a Victorian.

CONCLUSION

I began the Hip Santa Cruz History Project and website with the idea that the 1960s Hip Culture movement was a miracle. And even though it did not last, I still believe it was a miracle, and thus it proves that miracles (in the form of major cultural transformations) are possible. And thus, there may be some hope for our future on Planet Earth, despite all appearances to the contrary.

The story emerging in this volume details the arrival of this miraculous transformation in the words of some of the major players with whom I was personally acquainted. There are many others whom I did not know, and from whom I have no memoire to pass on.

The skeleton of this miracle story is a genealogy of artists, shown in this chart. I deeply regret that Ron Boise passed in 1966 before my arrival in Santa Cruz, and Charlie Nothing departed in 2007 without leaving me a story for this volume. However, he did leave an autobiography.

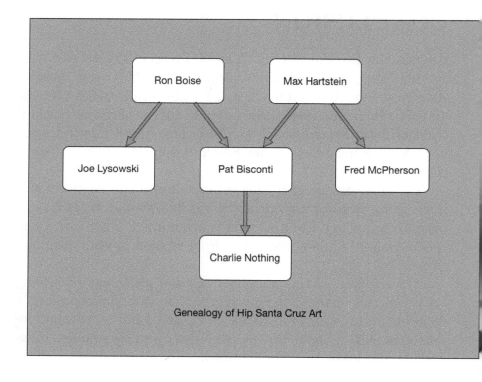

Genealogy of Hip Santa Cruz Art

References

Articles

- Dunn, Goeffrey (2015). What really happened 50 years ago in Santa Cruz at the first acid test. *Good Times of Santa Cruz*, December 2-8, 2015; pp. 22-37.

Books

- Harman, Holly (2015). *Inside a Hippie Commune: Holidays Commune, Santa Cruz Mountains & Beyond, circa 1964 to 1970s.* Healdsburg, CA: Harman Publishing.

- Simon, Charles Martin (2000). *The Life and Crimes of Charlie Nothing.* Soquel, CA: CM Simon.

- Wolfe, Tom (1969). *The Electric Kool-Aid Acid Test.* New York, NY: Farrar, Strauss and Giroux.

Websites

- Abraham, Ralph H. (2002) *The Hip Santa Cruz History Project.*
  http://www.ralph-abraham.org/1960s/

- Abraham, Ralph H., and Jacob Aman (2016) *The Hip Santa Cruz History Project.*
  http://hipsantacruz.org/

CPSIA information can be obtained
at www.ICGtesting.com
Printed in the USA
FSHW020515150119
55030FS